MUSIC AND SELF-MANAGEMENT METHODS

A Physiological Model

Joseph P. Scartelli, Ph.D., RMT-BC

MMB HORIZON SERIES

THE LOTUS FLOWER

Held sacred by the ancients in the Near and Far East, the lotus flower has an uninterrupted symbolic history of over 5,000 years. It is a symbol of hope, faith and renewed life as it closes its petals at night, sinking beneath the water, only to rise and open again with the sunrise.

This flower was chosen to represent this series as a symbol of our hope and faith in therapy, special education, rehabilitation medicine, the helping professions and in the development of individuals to their fullest potential.

MUSIC AND SELF- MANAGEMENT METHODS
A Physiological Model

Joseph P. Scartelli, Ph.D., RMT-BC

ISBN 0-918812-53-4

Cover Artwork: Mary Lynn Brophy
Printer: McNaughton and Gunn Lithographers, Inc.

ABOUT THE AUTHOR

Joseph P. Scartelli, Ph.D., RMT-BC received his undergraduate degree in music education from Mansfield University, Pennsylvania and his Master of Music Therapy and Ph.D. in music education/therapy from the University of Miami, Coral Gables, Florida. He has worked as a public school instrumental music teacher in Pennsylvania and Florida, and as a music therapist with cerebral palsied, socially maladjusted, emotionally disturbed, and developmentally disabled populations. Prior to his present position of Program Director of Music Therapy at Radford University, Radford, Virginia, he served as Chair of the Music Therapy Department at the University of Miami. He is presently involved in researching the application of music and biofeedback to relaxation training and stress management and researching the neurological effects of music. He is at work on numerous publications and presentations on those topics.

CONTENTS

INTRODUCTION

Approaches to health care have been experiencing a steady trend in the application of behavioral medicine and self-regulation strategies to physiological and psychological disorders.[1] Implied in the trend is the belief that, where appropriate and possible, recession from pharmacological treatment can be in the patient's best interest. Shapiro[2] points out that there is a growing concern about the adverse effects and misuse of medication treatments. Oddly enough, this trend survives (and thrives) in the face of extraordinary and unprecedented advances in medicine and medical technology including a rapid rate of discoveries about the brain and its many mechanisms – chemical, electrical, and hormonal.

As this knowledge grows, we become increasingly impressed with the potential of the brain including its homeostatic and physical defense/immune mechanisms. Subsequently, it becomes more evident that the patient can be trained to take greater responsibility for his or her health maintenance and recovery by learning to tap mechanisms that relax or excite, increase strength and endurance, increase powers of concentration, and allow our homeostatic systems (blood pressure, heart rate, body temperature, respiration, etc.) to operate at maximum efficiency. Spiegel and Spiegel[3] tell us that under the right circumstances, the mind and body have extraordinary control abilities, i.e., to increase strength and to withstand pain.

Among the possibilities now becoming commonplace, is the ability of a person to learn control of autonomic and less perceptible somatic functions of the body. This learning is particularly applicable in stress and pain management. Stress, as an architectural term, identifies an area where excessive pressure or force is exerted, resulting in a steady weakening of that area. In human behavior, stress occurs when external factors continue to act on an organism creating progressive maladapting reactions until imbalances in physical and psychological states become pathological.

As indicated by the flood of articles, books, and media coverage in the last two decades, stress is now recognized as a major factor in illness, both physical and psychological. The American Medical Association has stated that "at least 80% of all medical disorders are psychosomatic or stress related."[4] Astor[5] reinforces this line of thinking more conservatively by pointing out that an estimated 60 to 70% of medical disorders treated today are caused or aggravated by psychological involvement. How we think, our attitudes toward illness and disease and our attitudes regarding our involvement in the recovery process have become critical issues in health care and maintenance.

To a certain extent, the physical and psychological evolution of the human body simply have not kept pace with the societal and technological advances of modern times. Rosenbaum[6] states that the contemporary environment is associated with coronary heart disease by way of rewarding Type A behavior. This behavior is characterized by traits of aggressiveness, competitiveness, ambition and pressure associated with time and deadlines. He continues to point out that our modern civilization must cope with pressures of urbanization, population density and rapid technological progress never experienced by preceding generations. Levi[7] adds that "a great deal of urbanized, industrialized environment constitutes an insult – and a trauma – to man's neuroendocrine system, giving rise to mental and/or psychosomatic disease."

In addition to stressors that are the result of rapid technological advances, there are the old standbys which have always been with us: job stress, economic, family, educational and relationship difficulties which always seem to keep the pressure on. As these stressors become increasingly abundant, we must develop means to deal adequately with them and to maintain a psychological and physiological homeostasis while continuing to function appropriately by the definitions and demands of modern culture and society. Decreased ability to allow the body to recover from these accumulated stressors will result in disorders that include coronary heart disease, high blood pressure, depression, atherosclerosis, alcoholism, drug dependency and reduced resistance to common illnesses such as colds, and even cancer. Disease and in some cases, even death can follow negative life events such as grief, financial loss and humiliation. Vulnerability to infectious disease and cancer may be affected by how we react to stress.[8] Gatchel and Baum[9] acknowledging that stress can be a precursor to cancer, note that the mechanism involved appears to be a breakdown in the immune system which, under normal circumstances, will destroy pre-cancerous cells. When an event such as the death of a loved one occurs, this immune system weakens and may fail to detect and eliminate the cancerous cells.

A vast amount of clinical and research-based literature has been devoted to the prevention and treatment of stress-related disorders. All of this information, in one way or another, affirms the importance of learning to relax as a means of dealing with life's stressors. Indeed, thousands of books and articles are dedicated to dozens of methods to teach an individual to relax, particularly in the face of those events that would have one anguish. These techniques include meditation, hypnosis, imagery, autogenic therapy and biofeedback. Many of these methods are offered as alternatives to medication and even surgery.

In addition to these relaxation methods, a striking trend in the recognition of the application of music to combat stress is taking place. Obviously, we have all used music to relax, as a diversion and as a blocker of unwanted thoughts and sounds. This is one of the great attractions of music and we have simply taken for granted its ability to do these things. Advertisements of music for relaxation, imagery enhancers, etc. are abundant in lay and professional publications. Frankly, there are few aspects of our society that do not involve or include music implicitly or explicitly.

However, we can no longer allow music to be taken for granted in this application. It must be examined in an orderly fashion to maximize its effects, thus, joining the ranks of meditation, imagery, systematic desensitization, biofeedback, and so forth, as an addition to, and in combination with, these relaxation training methodologies. In doing so we must look at music as a less mystical or phenomenological entity and more as an acoustic and psychoacoustic event that acts on an individual's physical state, emotions, intellect and spirit almost always simultaneously.

Therefore, the purpose of the following chapters is first to discuss self-management techniques and effects, and secondly to examine the theoretical and practical foundations and applications of music as an agent in stress management and self-control. They will also investigate the work that has been conducted in the area of music and biofeedback for relaxation training. The information will be preceded by a discussion of stress and its physiology. It is hoped that health care professionals will benefit from the information concerning the organized and purposeful use of music and employ it where deemed appropriate in both training and treatment of stress-related disorders. The monograph is written in a review of literature format with the intention of giving the reader exposure to the researchers in the disciplines included in the topic. In addition, the author hopes that this collection of sources will provide a convenient reference for the furthering of research in this exciting and important area of therapy.

I PHYSIOLOGICAL AND PSYCHOLOGICAL CORRELATES OF STRESS

In recent decades, the professions of medicine and psychology have acknowledged the direct connection of the mind to the body (psyche to soma) with regard to disorders and diseases that occur in Man. Thus we see many branches of psychology and medicine devoted to the study and treatment of such disorder, i.e., psychosomatic medicine, holistic medicine, behavioral medicine, psychophysiological medicine, and physiological psychology. Green, et al.[10] point out that the psyche to soma principle implies that every change in the physiological state will effect a change in the psychological state while every change in the psychological state will effect a change in the physiological. During this last decade, as Gatchel and Baum report,[9] "psychological contributions to medically relevant topics have become an important part of medical science, with the growing interest in treating patients as 'whole' human beings and the realization that psychological factors are important in the course of almost any disease." (p.5) Indeed, a number of medical schools are following a trend which acknowledges this fact and have recently expanded admission standards placing less priority on the mathematics and science achievement and more on the nonscientific experiences of prospective medical students in an effort to produce competent physicians who would also show more compassion for the person behind the illness.[11]

As noted earlier, stress and anxiety can have deleterious effects on the health state or homeostasis of the human body. Selye[12] has formulated what he had termed the general adaption syndrome describing how people respond to stress. It "consists of three phases:

- an alarm reaction in response to the demands of a stress producing agent or stressor,
- resistance or adaption to the demands of the stressor,
- exhaustion or depletion of energy from continued exposure to the stressor." (p. 113)

The physiological responses to the general adaption syndrome include increased heart rate, blood pressure, respiration, skin temperature, sweat gland activity, gastrointestinal activity, pupillary changes and muscle tone. Selye continues by stating that this physiological arousal is also known as the "fight-flight" response which prepares the individual's body to deal with immediate imbalances caused by the environment.

The fight-flight response, a primitive reaction to stressors, is observed throughout the animal kingdom. It is manifested by an animal literally fighting or fleeing from an adversarial situation. This response, notes Benson[13] causes an increase in blood pressure, heart rate, muscle blood flow, and metabolism. The human being, however, does not automatically physically fight or flee from confrontal or adversive situations being, in this case, 'handicapped' with the ability to use intellect and reason, therefore remaining in the situation for extended and unhealthy lengths of time, i.e., in a situation of stressful employment, financial difficulties or problems in relationships, for example. Benson continues, "the fight or flight response, repeatedly elicited, may ultimately lead to the dire diseases of heart attack and stroke." (p. 25) We all possess a mechanism which can check overstress which Benson has called the 'relaxation response.' This response is "extremely simple if your follow a very short set of instructions which incorporate four essential elements:

- a quiet environment,
- a mental device such as a word or a phrase used over and over again,
- the adoption of a passive attitude, which is perhaps the most important of the elements,
- a comfortable position." (p. 27)

When properly practiced, a reduction of autonomic nervous system activity will result.

The brain receives and transmits information via an elegantly structured nervous system. The two major networks are the central and peripheral nervous systems. The central nervous system is made up of the spinal cord and brain. This system receives input from the peripheral nervous system, processes it, and formulates a reaction that instructs the peripheral nervous system response. The peripheral nervous system is responsible for communicating information from the senses, organs, tissues and muscles to the central nervous system creating a cyclic relationship between the two nervous systems. The peripheral nervous system is further divided into two major nerve networks, the autonomic and somatic nervous systems. The autonomic nervous system monitors and innervates the involuntary body functions while the somatic nervous system monitors and innervates the voluntary body functions.

Anderson[14] points out that the autonomic nervous system is made up of two antagonistic mechanisms, the sympathetic nervous system which effects arousal of the autonomic functions and the parasympathetic nervous system which is a tropotropic mechanism responsible for inhibiting activity of the sympathetic nervous system. Therefore, as Wolpe[15] states, the intent of relaxation training is to activate the parasympathetic nervous system. On the other hand, the somatic system, in addition to control of the striated musculature, provides the central nervous system with its only access to information from the external environment by way of sensory input. The central nervous system, therefore, has the ability to send messages out to the peripheral nerves, organs and muscles in response to this external information. Ultimately, all of these systems, interact and occasionally compete with one another in response to external and internal activity and change.

Another system of the body that should be recognized with regard to reactions to stress is the endocrine system. This is the chemical system which works in tandem with the nervous system releasing stimulative or sedative chemicals or hormones in reaction to external and internal events. Both the central nervous system and endocrine systems are mediated by the hypothalamus, an area of the brain that lies just above the brain stem and regulates most internal body functions such as blood flow, body temperature, organ function and metabolism.

The endocrine system consists of two sub-systems that have particular functions during exposure to stress. The first is called the catacholamines, chiefly consisting of two neurotransmitter hormones, epinephrine (adrenaline) and norepinephrine (noradrenaline). These chemical are released into the blood stream when activated by the adrenal medulla located just above the kidneys and work with the sympathetic nervous system contributing to increased heart rate, constriction of blood vessels and reduction of gastrointestinal activity. The second sub-system of the endocrine system is the corticosteroids. Also involved in reaction to stress, this system involves the hypothalamus, pituitary and adrenal cortex. When stimulated, the pituitary gland secretes adrenocorticotrophic hormone (ACTH) which in turn stimulates the adrenal cortex, thus controlling the secretion of the appropriate corticosteroids. Curtis[16] has shown that emotional stress appears to elevate corticosteroid levels with the initial intent of activating and maintaining muscular strength and endurance (the primitive response to prepare the body to fight or flee in response to danger). One secretion particularly involved with reactions to stress is cortisol which enters the blood stream as a result of external and internal imbalances of heat, cold and sympathetic stimulation. Cortisol speeds the body's access to stores of energy such as fats and carbohydrates, thus helping the body in its resistance to stress.[9] Selye[12] indicated that during the "alarm reaction" phase of the general adaption syndrome, the anterior pituitary gland secretes ACTH, activating the adrenal cortex to secrete additional hormones (cortisol). Hormone output during this stage is high. During the resistance stage, much of the physiological activity in the first stage terminates. In the third phase, exhaustion, the pituitary and adrenal cortex are drained of their output, leaving the body unguarded and resulting in severe physical exhaustion and possible death. Physiologically, one of the critical results of this syndrome is the reduced effectiveness of the body's immune system. Under these extreme conditions, lymphocytic activity is reduced, increasing susceptibility to infection, tumor development and even shrinking/atrophy of lymphocytic tissue.[17]

When a stressor is present for an extended period of time, the sympathetic and endocrine systems work overtime, maintaining arousal of the autonomic nervous system. The heart pumps harder and faster with greater resistance from the constricted arterial network (caused by the release of epinephrine and norepinephrine). The longer the stress is present, the greater the damage will be. Benson[13] notes that increased blood pressure requires the heart to pump more forcefully. The muscles fibers of the heart therefore increase, enlarging the heart. As the heart enlarges to pump, it requires more blood to nourish itself. In this vicious cycle, the heart eventually becomes increasingly undernourished resulting in inefficiency and weakening. The inevitable result is a heart attack. In addition to the heart, this cycle will also have deleterious consequences on other vital organs that are directly or indirectly affected by stress, such as the kidneys or brain, resulting in kidney disease or stroke, for instance.

Emotional and psychological factors have much to do with how we handle stress. Suinn[18] reminds us that psychosomatic symptoms are a result of physical reactions to stress and emotions. The physical reactions are not viewed as a psychological defense mechanism (such as is the case with conversion reaction), therefore, treatment must consider actual physical changes and alterations. Green and Green[19] concur, adding that psychosomatic disease is a medically undesirable physiological response to psychological stress. From the standpoint of treatment, the disorder exists in the body, not the head. Suinn lists ten types of psychophysiological reactions:

" • psychophysiologic skin reactions, e.g., neurodermatitis, or 'hives',
 • psychophysiologic musculoskeletal reactions, e.g., arthritis, backache, cramps,
 • psychophysiologic respiratory reaction, e.g., asthma, hayfever, sinusitis,
 • psychophysiologic cardiovascular reaction, e.g., hypertension, migraine, angina,
 • psychophysiologic hemic and lymphatic reactions, e.g. psychogenic hemorrhage,
 • psychophysiologic gastrointestinal reactions, e.g., ulcers, constipation,
 • psychophysiologic genitourinary reactions, e.g., certain menstrual disturbances,
 • psychophysiologic endocrine reactions, e.g., obesity, certain types of hypothyroidism,
 • psychophysiologic nervous system reactions, e.g., loss of strength,
 • psychophysiologic reactions of organs of special sense, e.g., vertigo." (p 252-253)

Weissburg[20] notes a sequence of behavior in response to stress in psychological terms. Stress leads to denial which is followed by episodes of disorganization and symptom formation. At this stage, disruption of psychological homeostasis occurs. In the next step of the sequence we see the development of maladaptive behaviors, examples of which include alcoholism, child abuse and suicide. At this point, the sequence has bottomed out and the individual must return to psychological equilibrium or remain in this pathologically disturbed state. Behavioral/psychological indicators of the stress response include restlessness, troubled sleep, hyperactivity, aggressive behavior, increased substance abuse, increased hypochondria behavior, anxiety, phobias, nightmares, concentration and memory problems, and complications with pre-existing psychiatric disorders. Cohen (cited in Gatchel and Baum[9]) notes that there are after-effects which result from exposure to a stressor. The more energy expended resisting the stressor, the greater the after-effects which include "decreased cognitive ability, reduced tolerance for frustration, aggressiveness, helplessness, decreased sensitivity to others, and withdrawal." (p. 72) These after-effects are to be expected, even if the person has successfully coped with the stressor. Physiologically, if a stressor continues to occur, is prolonged, or is joined by other stressors, the catecholamine levels in the brain deplete. Weick, *et al.* (cited in Gatchel and Baum[9]) have found, in animal studies, that this type of situation can very likely lead to death.

Perception of all of our functioning — intellectual, physical, psychological and even emotional takes place in the brain. Emotional activity resides in the mid- or paleomammalian portion of the brain. The areas specifically involved in emotion are collectively termed the limbic system. This collection of structures is located in the vicinity of the thalamus and hypothalamus. The nuclei that make up the limbic system are the septum, mamilliary bodies, hippocampus, amygdala, and cingulate cortex.[21] These areas transmit and receive information to and from the thalamus and hypothalamus.[22] As Benson[13] points out, the hypothalamus is actively involved in reactions to stress by initiating the secretion of catacholamines.

Some of these areas have specifically determined functions. For example, the amygdala is responsible for processing behaviors of rage, aggression and fear. The hippocampus also processes fear and rage, but not to the extent of the amygdala.[23] The actions of fight or flight occur with stimulation of the amygdala.[24] Damage to the areas of the cingulate cortex produced deficits in avoidance behavior.[24] Furthermore, it has been determined that opiate receptors, i.e., enkephalins and beta-endorphins, have been localized in the amygdala, among other brain centers. These morphine-like analgesics are stimulated by the limbic system. Additionally, beta-endorphins and ACTH are secreted in parallel by the anterior pituitary during stress.[21] Therefore, a great deal of activity takes place in the relatively small limbic area of the brain in reactions to stress. However, it has a profound effect on numerous body functions that ultimately give us the feelings we recognize as excitement, fear, discomfort, intensity and so on.

Buck[25] states that once a stressor presents itself and the knowledge of this reaches the brain, the appropriate cortical areas alert the amygdala and hypothalamus. The hypothalamus, being a central mediator of the processes involved with stress reaction, activates the autonomic nervous system which in turn stimulates the adrenal medulla to release epinephrine and norepinephrine. The hypothalamus also activates the anterior pituitary which releases ACTH thus stimulating the adrenal cortex to release corticoids (steroid hormones), all to prepare the body for defense against the stressor. Limbic signals, state Green and Green,[19] are essentially converted to autonomic and hormonal signals through the transducing machinery of the hypothalamus and pituitary. Levinthal[21] in tying these systems together concludes, "the circumstantial evidence leads to a strong suspicion that analgesia, stress, emotionality and endorphine systems might be somehow interconnected." (p. 357)

The preceding description of the nervous and endocrine systems' reactions to stress were presented to give the reader an introduction to the physiological changes that result from exposure to stressors that affect the organs, muscles, and ultimately behavior. As external events can affect the internal state, a number of self-management methods are being utilized in the clinic to override these effects. These methods can control changes in the internal state thereby helping the patient to be less helpless in the battle to maintain psychological and physical homeostasis. The following chapter will discuss a number of the more popular methods, examining their respective concepts, techniques and results. It is important to remember that as individuals use these methods to combat stress and learn to relax, they are activating the nervous and endocrine systems to their favor in an effort to obtain a healthy psychological and physiological state.

II SELF-MANAGEMENT METHODOLOGIES

The self-management methods to be described in this section have all enjoyed success in application to stress management. They are noninvasive and require the patient to learn the techniques, subsequently resulting in learning to control body functions not normally within the somatic repertoire. In practicing these techniques, we acknowledge that the human being can learn to control both autonomic and somatic functions with the proper training. The most common methods are hypnosis and self-hypnosis, autogenic therapy, imagery, meditation, progressive relaxation, behavioral conditioning methods such as systematic desensitization, and biofeedback.

Hypnosis and Self-Hypnosis

Hypnosis and self-hypnosis are enjoying continued popularity as serious procedures to relax and cope with stressful stimuli.[26] Adams[27] defines hypnosis as an altered state of consciousness while also maintaining a state of hypersuggestibility. He continues, stating that hypnosis and self-hypnosis are one and the same in that the only difference is that in heterohypnosis the hypnotist guides your thoughts, whereas in self-hypnosis you guide your own thoughts. Basically, all hypnosis is self-hypnosis. Spiegel and Spiegel[3] point out that the hypnotic state is not one of sleep, but one of wakefulness and alertness. Zibbergeld, et al.[28] add that there are no known physiological correlates to distinguish hypnosis from relaxation or meditation.

Physiologically, hypnosis correlates with relaxation where relaxation will reduce autonomic and somatic activity. However, as Negley-Parker[29] points out, there is no specific or unique cause and effect relationship of hypnosis and physiology. It is commonly known, of course, that a subject can learn to change and control physical states through suggestion. However, there are no innate or unusual physical differences between the restful waking state and the hypnotic state.

Hypnosis is being applied in medicine with greater frequency, particularly as an anesthetic. Long[30] notes that it can ease suffering due to pain and also speed healing. In addition to pain control, hypnotherapy has been found to be appropriate for nausea, skin disorders, autonomic and endocrine disorders and anxiety.

Pratt[31] stresses that hypnosis and self-hypnosis are useful in stress management. The goal of hypnosis is relaxation. "Whether one chooses to call it relaxation therapy, autogenic training, meditation or progressive relaxation is immaterial - the techniques are hypnotic." (p. 322) In essence, relaxation induced by hypnosis reduces the effects of stress by changing the patient's perception of and reaction to the stressor. Peterfy[32] cautions that hypnosis is not a panacea, but when appropriately and prudently applied, it has a place in medical treatment, helping to bring about temporary and even permanent relief from numerous psychosomatic disorders.

Autogenic Therapy

Autogenic or self-directed therapy was developed by Schultz and Luthe[33] as a passive-relaxation technique. In general, it involves a "self-induced psychophysiological shift to a specific state (autogenic state) which facilitates autogenic (brain-directed, self-generated, self-regulatory) processes of self-normalizing nature. In other words, autogenic training and related autogenic approaches are designed to promote and to give specifically adapted support to those brain-directed, self-regulatory (autogenic) mechanisms which normally participate in homeostatic, recuperative and self-normalizing processes ... the physiological and psychophysiological oriented effects of autogenic approaches may be considered as being diametrically opposed to changes elicited by stress." (p. 1) Using this approach, the patient assumes the bulk of the responsibility for carrying out his or her own treatment by performing prescribed mental exercises. When correctly practiced, a psychophysiological shift occurs from a normal state to the autogenic state. This shift produced significant reductions of afferent and efferent impulses.

Anderson[14] points out that autogenic therapy is a passive or nonmuscular relaxation technique which includes six standard exercise areas: heaviness, warmth, cardiac regulation, respiration, abdominal warmth, and cooling of the forehead. Additionally it includes seven mental exercises: spontaneous experience of colors, experience of selected of colors, visualization of concrete objects, visualization of abstract objects, experience of a selected state of feeling, visualization of other persons, and answers from the unconscious.

A functional premise of autogenic therapy is that the brain, like other organs in the body, has mechanisms to maintain homeostasis, in this case mental. This premise assumes that when an individual experiences excesses in stress or other disturbing mental stimuli, the brain has the ability to engage physical processes (biological) to reduce the disturbance. This reduction is termed neutralization.[34]

Imagery

Imagery as a relaxation method holds some similarities to autogenic therapy. Its format, however, is less structured. The use of imagery for the purposes of promoting relaxation requires the patient to produce a mental image accompanied by physical sensation. The mental pictures evoked during imagery can be free-running and shaped by the subject or they can be set up or led by a therapist, as in guided imagery.

The human nervous system communicates with two internal languages. Verbal thoughts must communicate directly with the somatic nervous system. For example, if you wish to stand up, all you need to do is think "stand up" and the voluntary nervous system and corresponding voluntary musculature respond appropriately. Conversely, imagery directly accesses the autonomic nervous system which, of course, regulates the involuntary body functions.[35] The authors provide an example of this idea. First using verbal commands, tell yourself to produce an excess of saliva. They hypothesize that very little saliva will be produced by this command. However, if one was to imagine a juicy lemon cut open, imagine its smell, imagine biting into a slice of the lemon, imagine your cheeks and lips curling and puckering, then the saliva production response is much more likely, particular with practice.

This mechanism can be important in the treatment of psychological and physiological disorders. Turk[36] states that a patient's cognitive systems dictate a mental set which contributes to the successful coping of a disorder or illness. How a person experiences health, symptoms and illness, what they mean to him or her, and how these meanings influence behavior are all integral parts of health and disease when viewed as a total human response. An individual's belief system has a direct effect on his/her health care, maintenance and recovery. Following this line of thinking, Jaffe and Bressler[35] note that if a patient dwells on pain, giving it descriptions such as "a hot poker sticking in my back," he reinforces the sensation of pain. He also contributes to a feeling of increased helplessness with respect to the pain. "When the imagination is preoccupied by these negative pictures, the autonomic nervous system is being told, in effect, 'prepare the body to be helpless'." (p. 255) However, a positive image can reverse the psychological and physical effects. Jaffe and Bressler point out that while in a dentist's chair, a patient can reduce gum bleeding through training in imagery. They cite that several dentists have reported success when directing their patients to imagine that ice was being applied to the bleeding gums. Patients report that a numbing sensation occurs, however, the blood vessels also constrict thus reducing the bleeding. The fact is that no physical disorder is unaffected by the mind. A positive set of images enhances and speeds healing, whereas depression and helplessness can provide obstacles for the process. Additionally, anyone can be taught to use imagery for therapeutic value and with practice can make it very effective in managing stress and illness. Norris[37] reinforces the potential of imagery by reminding us that it is the trigger for all voluntary physical tasks and, with practice, can be very powerful in increasing volition.

Meditation

Meditation is another popular means to relax, thus reducing the adverse symptoms of stress. Gaining popularity in the sixties and seventies, it is practiced in many forms including Zen, Yoga and Transcendental Meditation. When practiced correctly, an altered state of consciousness is accomplished with accompanying hypometabolic changes in body function.[38] Norvell[39] describes the procedure for transcendental meditation as an example:

1) A quiet area is needed where there will be no interruptions;
2) A comfortable position is necessary to achieve total muscle relaxation;
3) A mantra must be repeated aloud or mentally concentrating all attention to the work;
4) One must breathe deeply and rhythmically with the eyes closed;
5) visualize a scene that can help maintain the relaxed state and not allow disturbing thoughts to surface.

Bloomfield, *et al.*[40] point out that the practice of meditation can reduce accumulated stress, increase body resistance to stress and nurture a state of psychophysiological integration. Goleman (cited in Bakel[41]) notes that meditators show a faster recovery time from a stressor than nonmeditators.

The hypometabolic state previously referred to is also known as the relaxation response. Physiologically, a meditative state is antagonistic to sympathetic nervous system activity. In research, it was found that experienced meditators were capable of reducing oxygen consumption and carbon dioxide production, reducing respiration rate, heightening galvanic skin response and increasing alpha wave state by 10 − 15% (Wallace and Benson, cited in Bakel[41]). Bakel[41] reveals that regular practice of transcendental meditation, many times, is responsible for acting as a catalyst for life-style change away from Type A characteristics. In fact, this life-style change of avoiding Type A behavior characteristics is a principal behavioral prescription for hypertension and its accompanying physical disorders.

The relaxation methods discussed to this point are generally categorized as passive concentration or passive relaxation techniques, somewhat of a "mind over matter" approach. Progressive muscle relaxation, although requiring a good deal of mental concentration to work effectively, is the one method that necessitates awareness of the voluntary musculature (skeletal muscle). It is an active relaxation inasmuch as the various sections of the body work actively in tandem with the mind. Whereas imagery and autogenic therapy teach the patient to visualize or imagine sensations, progressive muscle relaxation involves the body physically in the relaxation process, a possible reason for its widespread popularity and clinical use.

Progressive Muscle Relaxation Training

Edmond Jacobson is considered the pioneer of the clinical application of self-controlled muscle relaxation as a treatment for symptoms of stress. Jacobson[42] states that tension causes the shortening of muscle fibers while relaxation creates a direct physiological opposite of nervous tension or excitement. Therefore, tension cannot be felt when the muscle fibers are in a lengthened state as a result of the relaxation procedure. In Jacobson's technique of progressive muscle relaxation, a person is taught to relax each major muscle group in the body in a sequenced manner until the entire body is in a deeply relaxed state.

Bernstein and Borkevec[43] describe the basic procedure of progressive muscle relaxation. The order of muscle groups to be relaxed is:

"   • dominant hand and forearm,
    • dominant bicep,
    • nondominant hand and forearm,
    • nondominant bicep,
    • forehead,
    • upper cheeks and nose,
    • lower cheeks and jaw,
    • neck and throat,
    • chest, shoulders and upper back,
    • abdominal or stomach region,
    • dominant thigh,
    • dominant calf,
    • dominant foot,
    • nondominant thigh,
    • nondominant calf,
    • nondominant foot." (p. 25)

The procedural sequence for each of these muscle groups is:

"   • the client's attention should be focused on the muscle group,
    • at a predetermined signal from the therapist, the muscle group is tensed,
    • tension is maintained for a period of 5 — 7 seconds (shorter for the feet),
    • at a predetermined cue, the muscle group is released,
    • the client's attention is maintained upon the muscle group as it relaxes." (p. 25)

This sequence should be conducted in an environment conducive to relaxation. With proper practice, an individual can be expected to achieve greater degrees of physical relaxation.

Behavior Therapies

Behavior therapy, in its many forms, acknowledges that behavior is very much a product of the individual's interaction with the environment. Behavior therapy is divided into two categories. Classical or respondent conditioning, as articulated by Pavlov, is the phenomenon of a stimulus eliciting a response (usually involving an involuntary reaction). The classic example, of course, is the Pavlovian experiment pairing the ringing bell with the presentation of meat to produce salivation in dogs. Once the animals have learned the association of the bell and meat, they would eventually salivate at the sound of the bell, a stimulus that under normal conditions would have little or no action upon the salivary mechanism. Classical conditioning, in short, states that our behavior is influenced by its antecedents.

Conversely, operant conditioning states that behavior is influenced by its consequents. The consequents may be either positive (thus increasing the future frequency of that behavior) or negative (thus decreasing the future frequency of that behavior). For the purposes of this present work, and because of the wealth of information available on classical and operant conditioning, there is no need to discuss these theories in greater detail. However, there are two relaxation training techniques that are based on these respective principles of behavior.

Systematic desensitization, developed by Joseph Wolpe, is a method for the treatment of the effects of stress and based on the principles of classical conditioning. Walker[44] states that systematic desensitization is a sequence of activities which condition the subject to pair feelings of relaxation with an anxiety producing stimulus to deal with the symptoms of stress. This procedure is similar to the pairing of the bell with the presentation of meat to produce activation of the involuntary mechanism of salivation.

Wachtel[45] describes the procedure of systematic desensitization. First, the stimuli which evoke the patient's anxiety are located. Second, one or more hierarchies are drawn up where the patient's fears are recognized from slight to intense. It is in the third stop where the patient is trained in deep muscle relaxation. Once the relaxation has been attained, the patient is asked to imagine the first (least anxiety causing) item on the hierarchy. The therapist slowly guides the patient up the hierarchy, maintaining the deeply relaxed state. Wachtel adds that there is practical value in using the imagined scenes to arouse anxiety since no one therapist could possess all the stimuli needed to act as a catalyst for stress. With proper guidance, there is a variety of stimuli which can be imagined by the patient, with a great range of intensity to be utilized and manipulated by the therapist. Systematic desensitization has enjoyed a high level of popularity and success not only for the treatment of stress and anxiety produced disorders, but also for pain management and phobia therapy.

III BIOFEEDBACK

Biofeedback techniques are the most objective approaches for training and maintaining relaxation. Biofeedback is one of the purest manifestations of operant condition insomuch that the technique is directly aimed at a response conditioned by consequential information provided by the biofeedback instrument. Although the functions of the autonomic nervous system are usually considered under the privy of classical conditioning (involuntary responses), through the use of biofeedback technology these autonomic functions can now be consciously controlled within an empirical framework thus allowing themselves to be affected via the operant conditioning technique of biofeedback.

Biofeedback, according to Wickramasekera,[46] is a training procedure that allows a person to alter physiological and bioelectrical events occurring within the body. The bases of the biofeedback technique are:

" • continuous and accurate monitoring of the physiological response to be altered,
  • immediate feedback to the subject of changes in the response,
  • motivation to alter the response." (p. 7)

The motivation to alter the response, in operant terms, is positive reinforcement. The biofeedback procedures allow the subject to see or hear a direct indication of the physiological response to be monitored. In fact, biofeedback is an extremely efficient form of operant conditioning where the training produces control of the subliminal responses more rapidly, establishes higher response rates, and yields voluntary cessation or change in activity more quickly than known operant conditioning techniques. Therefore, biofeedback can be associated with operant conditioning, instrumental learning, or trial and error. When the subject responds correctly, he or she is rewarded. In the case of biofeedback, it is the desired change in auditory or visual response of the instrument that provides the reward. For instance, if one learns to lower blood pressure, the biofeedback instrument tone will concurrently decrease, giving the patient concrete and rewarding information to show him/her that (s)he is on the right track. Wolf[47] does point out a difference in standard operant conditioning techniques and biofeedback. The tone or visual response of the biofeedback reinforcement is precise and continuous whereas operant reinforcement is often discontinuous, delayed and intermittent.

Fuller[48] notes that biofeedback uses electronic instrumentation designed to mirror psychophysiological processes of which we are not readily aware. Through visual and/or auditory feedback produced by the instrumentation, an individual can be made first aware of the level of functioning of these previously imperceptible physical activities and, secondly, learn to alter these activities subsequently through the new information provided by the electronic feedback.

The electronic devices detect minute, normally imperceptible physiological functions by way of electrodes. The electrodes, much like microphones, send the detected impulses to the biofeedback instrument which, among other functions, amplifies the signal and converts it to an auditory and/or visual signal which can be perceived by the patient. This signal is proportional to the level of activity being monitored. For example, if muscle tone is the target activity, the greater the tension the higher and louder the pitch and conversely, the less muscle tension present in the patient the lower and softer the pitch. Astor[5] adds that the three main goals in biofeedback therapy are awareness, control, and transfer. If one is to relieve muscle tension, for instance, one must be aware of the anxiety, stress and mental states that accompany it. (This statement acknowledges the role of the limbic system activity in relaxation.) A cycle is given as an example:

- the patient experiences tension,
- the feedback device informs the patient via amplification and transmission of tension signals, thus making the patient aware of location and intensity of the tension,
- with the given information, through mental devices and internal manipulation, the patient is able to control the function in question, such as heart rate, blood pressure, muscle tension, or skin temperature,
- the desired state is achieved and the feedback system is completed,
- the patient is relieved and homeostasis of the mind and body is achieved.

FIGURE I
Normally Imperceptible Activity

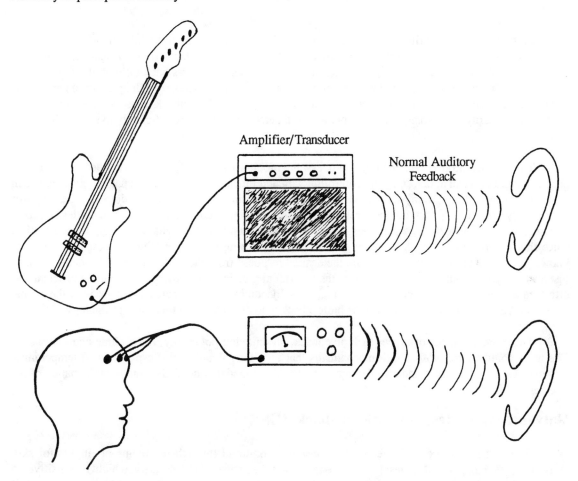

Figure I – As the guitar amplifier allows one to hear an electric guitar, the biofeedback instrument detects (via electrodes) imperceptible physiological activity, amplifies it and allows one to hear that information. When an individual can hear the guitar, (s)he therefore has the 'feedback' necessary to determine right from wrong notes and use that information to improve. Similarly, when an individual can hear previously imperceptible physiological activity, (s)he also has the feedback necessary to consciously change that activity in a desired direction. In both cases, the feedback is information which has been transduced so that it can communicate via a normal communication sense, in this case hearing.

As Green and Green[19] state, this simple feedback loop is highly significant. By using the biofeedback, "many unconscious and involuntary processes, having formerly sent signals only to the hypothalamus, now give feedback signals to the cortex. Closing this biocybernetic loop means bridging the normal gap between conscious and unconscious processes, voluntary and involuntary, and voluntary self-regulation through employment of imagination and visualization." (p. 213)

Sargent[49] states that external stressors create cognitive and affective responses via simultaneous activation of cortical and limbic systems, respectively. This, in turn, activates the hypothalamus which then activates the pituitary-hormonal axis, finally creating a defensive state in the autonomic nervous system (as discussed earlier). Proper biofeedback application provides the patient with objective data to become aware of, and subsequently the ability to control targeted functions of the autonomic and somatic nervous systems. The patient perceives a reversal of stress reaction with direct perception of this physiological change. Positive changes effect the cortical and limbic systems which are perceived as cognitive and affective state changes. A principle goal of biofeedback, therefore, is the acquisition of learned control over the somatovicseral system, with particular emphasis on control of these organs active in patterns of emotional arousal.[50]

Biofeedback is primarily a strategy of learning. The patient, through the information presented by the biofeedback instrument, gains a heightened perception and awareness of previously undetectable functions. With this information, (s)he can learn to control those functions back through the biofeedback instrument. This results in an accelerated and more efficient learning process regarding relaxation and stress management when compared to other forms of relaxation therapy. Biofeedback-assisted relaxation training does not necessarily teach something new, but allows a person to relax more efficiently in relatively shorter periods of time.

To complete properly the treatment process, the monitoring apparatus is slowly faded as the patient becomes more efficient at detecting and controlling targeted functions. Note that the patient must engage in some sort of mental and/or physical activity to bring about a shift in the monitored domain. Examples of this activity are imagery, deep muscle relaxation, and breathing technique. Patients, with the help of a therapist, experiment with these activities to determine which ones, and in what forms, are most effective. Once this discovery is made, the patient goes through a learning process in which (s)he gains increased knowledge of what (s)he must do to obtain the desired response from the biofeedback instrument. As with just about anything that is learned, the more the individual practices this procedure, the more efficient and effective the response. In the course of training, the subject must become increasingly aware of the mental images and/or strategies used to control the biofeedback thereby controlling their own physiology.

There are a number of modes of biofeedback, all enjoying popularity in the clinic and laboratory. The most common are biofeedback mechanisms that monitor galvanic skin response, skin temperature, brain waves, blood pressure and muscle tone. The choice of modality depends largely on the nature of the disorder.

Galvanic Skin Response Biofeedback (GSR)

Galvanic skin response biofeedback is usually monitored through the palms or fingers for skin resistance, an indicator of arousal. It is a reflection of sweat gland activity which is sensitive to sympathetic nervous system arousal. When one is calm and relaxed, skin resistance is high, whereas when one is under stress, skin resistance will decrease. Confusion sometimes arises when the GSR instrument is in operation. As the patient relaxes, skin resistance increases, however, the tone of the biofeedback instrument will decrease and vise versa. The goal, therefore, is to reduce and eventually eliminate the tone produced by the GSR, thus reducing sympathetic nervous system activity in the process. This process results in an overall feeling of relaxation that has been initiated, maintained, and controlled entirely by the mind of the patient. One can already see the potential for decreasing dependence on pharmacological intervention.

Thermal Biofeedback

A similar mode to GSR biofeedback is skin temperature or thermal feedback. The premise of thermal biofeedback is based on the fact that most persons can learn to control the surface skin temperature (usually the hands) simply by thinking about it. Warm hands usually indicate a state of relaxation while cold hands are a product of tension. As noted earlier, vasal constriction is a result of sympathetic nervous system activity.

The average person cannot distinguish temperature changes in the hands of less than three degrees. With the aid of the thermal biofeedback instrument, increments of 0.001 degrees Fahrenheit can be detected and communicated to the patient via the auditory and/or visual response thus allowing the patient many hundred times greater sensitivity to temperature change than normal.

Although there are numerous reports of the successful application of thermal biofeedback for migraine pain, Gatchel and Baum[9] caution that many of these studies have inadequate samples, designs and statistical analysis, casting some speculation on the technique until such time that more extensive and thorough research is conducted. In spite of this, however, thermal biofeedback continues to be a popular treatment avenue for migraine.

Electroencephalographic Biofeedback (EEG)

Electroencephalographic (EEG) biofeedback or brain wave training is a method of learning to elicit and subsequently control arousal of brain cells at a specific area of the brain. For relaxation purposes, it has been determined that the inhibition of substantial amounts of brain cells has a sedative effect on the autonomic and somatic nervous systems.

Brain wave frequencies are listed in four categories;
- beta (14 and above cycles/seconds or Hertz) — is considered a highly active state,
- alpha (8 — 13 Hz) — is characterized as the alert-relaxed state,
- theta (4 — 7 Hz) — is a state of pre-sleep,
- delta (0 — 3.5 Hz) — is the brain activity level of deep sleep.

In addition to the measurement parameter of frequency, brain waves must also be measured in terms of their power or amplitude (measured in microvolts). The brain wave is the result of asynchronous electrical firings of millions of cells. Depending on the amount and intensity of cell firings, an overall wave is produced. Therefore, if one is engaged in a highly active endeavor, such as performing a difficult piece on the piano, a proportionately large number of brain cells will be active resulting in a relatively higher frequency and amplitude. Lubar[51] notes that the full range of brain wave frequency is less than 1 to 40 Hz with an amplitude range of less than 2 to over 150 microvolts.

Kuhlman and Kaplan[52] explain the general relationship between some aspects of brain electrical activity and associated behavioral states. Additionally, biofeedback training is effective in the modification or control of EEG patterns. However, EEG activity is extremely complex. Known orderly relationships between EEG activity and behavior are few. It is also noted that EEG is the most elaborate of the biofeedback modalities due mostly to the extreme complexity of the brain and its electrical activity.

Brainwave activity is detected by electrodes placed at specified sites on the scalp. The EEG biofeedback usually functions with two electrodes (monopolar) or three electrodes (biopolar). The monopolar configuration consists of a reference (or ground) electrode and a recording (or active) electrode placed at a target site of the head. In the biopolar configuration, one reference electrode is now accompanied by two active electrodes placed at two target sites on the head. Because the EEG is sensitive to very small amounts of electricity, external electrical fields such as those produced by a nearby lamp or radio, can produce artifacts which create bogus readings that contaminate the authentic EEG activity of the brain. To accommodate this problem, all biofeedback units are now equipped with electronic filter systems that reject external interferences.

It is important to realize, according to Lubar[51] that EEG recorded at sites on the scalp of humans represents only the tip of the iceberg. Additionally, conditioning an EEG pattern in one individual might represent different processes when compared to the next. Variations in sub-cortical and brainstem activity probably account for most of this. It also helps to explain why subjective reports of patients in the alpha range vary so much.

The most popular application of EEG biofeedback is alpha wave training which has repeatedly been shown to accompany a quiet, relaxed, nondrowsy state with the eyes closed. The 'alpha state' is manifested by relaxed alertness, passive attention and mental relaxation. The resulting mental state is similar to that achieved in the successful practice of meditation, yoga and autogenic therapy. Stoyva and Kamiya[53] reveal that subjects in an alpha state report relaxation with the absence of visual imagery. Long periods of alpha activity were reported to be very pleasant. This state is also generally believed to be incompatible with the experience of pain, anxiety, depression and stress. The most popular therapeutic applications of EEG biofeedback are in relaxation training, treatment of chronic headache and pain, insomnia, phobias and epilepsy. The use of EEG feedback to train the normalization of the brain wave patterns of patients with seizure disorders has demonstrated substantial potential.

Interestingly, Plotkin[54] concludes from a review of the literature, the EEG alpha brain wave training does not necessarily produce better results in brain wave control than nonbiofeedback techniques. This is not all bad news though. It tells us that we already have this capacity "built-in" and this ability is only confirmed by the EEG biofeedback technique. Additionally, the EEG does have an empirical or objective dimension that the other techniques cannot offer providing added advantages to both therapist and patient.

Electromyography (EMG)

The form of biofeedback that enjoys the majority of application in the clinic and popularity in the research literature is electromyographic (EMG) biofeedback. EMG biofeedback provides instant or immediate information to the therapist and patient concerning imperceptible muscle activity. To be specific, electromyography deals with the monitoring of the electrical potentials produced by muscles, particularly the striated, voluntary musculature.[55]

This electrical activity produced by the muscles is measured in microvolts. Even at rest, most skeletal muscles will produce approximately 3 to 6 microvolts. Because any striated (skeletal) muscle site can be monitored, there are many applications and many more disorders that may be treated with EMG biofeedback as compared to the other formats of biofeedback. In general, EMG feedback will be used to train the patient to either increase or decrease muscle activity depending on the disorder.

Four considerations must be taken into account during EMG biofeedback training. Initially, the subject must be made aware of his or her muscle activity. Secondly, the subject must learn to increase or decrease muscle activity as described. Thirdly, the positive reinforcement of the feedback (provided by the biofeedback instrument) must be continuous. Finally, the newly acquired muscle skills must be used to perform a greater range of motion.[56] In agreement, Morris[57] adds that in biofeedback training, the subject must first internalize it, and then practice that skill to obtain the target performance.

The EMG can be an accurate reflection of the motor unit with a minimum of technical difficulties. Each twitch of a muscle fiber lasts approximately 9 milliseconds. After each excitation, the fibers of the motor unit are relaxed completely and are activated again only when the motor neuron transmits the command along the nerve fiber. Individual muscles of the body consist of hundreds of motor units and it is the summation of this activity that creates voluntary and involuntary fluctuation of tension and relaxation of the entire muscle.[58]

As noted earlier, the amplitude of a motor unit firing is measured in microvolts. The motor units twitch repetitively and asynchronously. This randomization of firings cause the smooth, rather than jerky, tension of the entire muscle. As a reference, it would take the action of two or three motor units to produce a barely noticeable twitch of the thumb.

A basic design or application of EMG biofeedback is described by Basmajian.[59] Upon placement of the electrodes over the desired muscle area, the subject need only be given general instructions. The subject is asked to contract the muscle under study while seeing and hearing the response of the biofeedback instrument. Shortly, the subject will be able to adjust to the sensitivity of the equipment and accept these responses as new form of proprioception. No prior experience or practice is required and, with proper guidance from the therapist, the most naive subject can soon learn to control muscles based on the information returned from the monitors. This practice can be used to control an area as large as an entire muscle or as small as a single motor unit. As an example, Basmajian describes the ability of all sixteen patients involved in a study monitoring the right pollicus brevis (at the base of the thumb) to control muscle contraction at will. In fact, the control was so pronounced that various rhythms could be produced by the isolated muscle including gallops and rolls.

Through the use of biofeedback training, one can first detect minute changes in muscle tone, and subsequently improve control of those muscles. Because many of these changes fall outside the realm of conscious control, mental maneuvers are developed and used to help bring about control of muscle tone. These maneuvers vary widely, probably as much as there are patients who use biofeedback. As the patient learns the biofeedback process, (s)he literally continues to search, through trial and error, to find particular mental images, thoughts, mind sets, etc. that produce the desired peripheral response. Therefore, as Adler and Adler[60] point out, the patient has a number of stimuli that (s)he must deal with mentally at one time or another during biofeedback training. First, the patient must be aware of proprioceptive and visceroceptive sensations, the fluctuating signals emitted by the biofeedback instrument in response to the patient's actual physical activity, and the achievement of a target sensation which is summoned from a memory of what the desired physical state feels like. In addition, the patient must invariably use images that are intentionally evoked with the goal of making the memory of the target sensation more vivid. (As will be discussed later, music can be applied as a cue to evoke specific recollections.) Finally, the patient must deal with intruding images or thoughts that seem to drift into consciousness at times during training. An examination of the combination of biofeedback with other procedures which can help the patient control the mental processes that are engaged in relaxation training will be discussed later.

In general, the procedure for training relaxation using EMG biofeedback is composed of six steps.
- Inform the subject as to the function of the biofeedback, what it does and does not do, how it will be applied, and how (s)he can use it.
- Apply the electrodes and allow the subject to freely experiment with the biofeedback device referring to the information given in the above step and addressing additional questions. The subject must be permitted to learn what makes the instrument response increase and decrease as a result of a deliberate muscular action (develop an awareness of the cause and effect relationship between the monitored muscle and the feedback). This should be done in a relaxed atmosphere. In this step, suggestions could be given to the subject concerning basic strategies such as breathing and imagery, for example, to increase control of the physiological system.
- When the subject indicates comfort with the device and knowledge of its function, a baseline must be taken. The baseline must be recorded without feedback to the patient and should be established over a number of sessions prior to training.
- Assuming that all preparation has been adequately completed, begin training in which the subject is now allowed the feedback from the instrument as an indicator of the level of muscle activity. Training sessions should initially run for approximately fifteen to thirty minutes per session. As the subject becomes increasingly efficient and successful at controlling the feedback, encourage awareness of the physical and mental processes and strategies (s)he is using to bring about that desired response.

- Begin fading the use of the biofeedback apparatus as the desired level of response becomes consistent. In the course of the fading phase, continue emphasis on awareness of the previously discussed physical and mental processes.
- Initiate closure, in which the subject demonstrates conscious control of the muscle.

It is essential that the goal of EMG biofeedback-assisted relaxation training remain the ability to elicit a relaxation response at will, and ultimately without biofeedback, since an instrument will not normally be available in everyday life situations where stressors often occur with little warning. Depending on the condition and the individual, maintenance sessions may be required to sustain the relaxation abilities and skills obtained in training. For excellent, detailed guidelines for current EMG research and application, the reader is referred to Fridlund and Cacioppo.[61]

The present literature, for the most part, tends to conclude that relaxation of no single muscle site on the human body has a generalizing effect on the remainder of the body, and studies using frontalis (forehead) relaxation confirm this. Additionally, Alexander and Smith[62] conclude that although the research literature is enthusiastic about biofeedback, most of these studies have serious shortcomings in design and statistical analysis. Additionally, there has been little control for the phenomenon of the placebo effect.

The efficacy of biofeedback has been questioned with regard to actual change directly attributable to biofeedback as opposed to change due to the placebo effect. Such factors as therapist bias, subject expectancy and demand characteristics may, as in other forms of therapy, be present in biofeedback therapy.[63]

In spite of what appears to be valid concerns about the efficacy of biofeedback, Lacy[64] states that in the long run the question of whether biofeedback has any specific effects over other methods of relaxation training is not crucially important. Research should be more concerned with determining how these techniques produce their effects, regardless of how small or temporary. Research is also needed to understand better the underlying neurophysiological processes that mediate these effects. To support this stand, Sharpley and Rogers[65] conducted a data meta-analysis revealing that EMG frontalis biofeedback was significantly superior to control studies using alternative relaxation procedures. These procedures, while effective, were not significant according to the investigators' findings.

Additional support for the efficacy of biofeedback has been shown in its cost effectiveness within the treatment milieu. Many proponents for biofeedback point out that, in addition to enhancing existing techniques for increasing somatic and autonomic control, it also increases time quality and cost effectiveness. Blanchard et al.[66] reported remarkable reductions in medical expenses of patients undergoing treatment for chronic headache. Within the declared limitations of the survey, the investigators report the average costs of forty-five patients for the two years prior to applications of combinations of relaxation and biofeedback training to be approximately $955. For the two years after the completion of this training, the average costs fell to approximately $52 per patient.

A good deal of research has been conducted testing the effects of biofeedback in combination with other relaxation methods. Stoyva[67] suggests that combining the advantages of biofeedback, such as its objectivity and physiological control, with other techniques such as autogenic therapy has four additional advantages. First, combining methods lessens the possibility of the patient becoming overly reliant on the biofeedback instrumentation. Secondly, biofeedback instruments can break down. Familiarizing the patient with other relaxation techniques will always provide a good backup. Thirdly, biofeedback addresses physiological parameters with little or no implicit mechanisms for developing the cognitive strategies that ultimately produce the relaxation. Finally, muscle relaxation training has little effect on the autonomic components of the anxiety which is at the root of the stress and tension. With particular respect to EMG-assisted relaxation training, Morris[57] adds that when the goal of therapy is to increase hypotonicity (reduction of muscle tone), all patients will not respond equally well and some may find it necessary to supplement the training with other techniques and procedures to aid in the relaxation training process.

Patel and North[68] obtained highly significant decreases in the systolic and diastolic blood pressure of hypertensive patients by combining GSR and EMG biofeedback with yoga meditation techniques. In discussing their rationale for using this combination, they state the "biofeedback has two components. The first is objective, and depends on showing changes in a physiological function as displayed by auditory or visual signals. The second is thought to be a subjective state which cannot be monitored." (p. 95)

Stoyva[67] notes that combining biofeedback with autogenic therapy provides an effective tandem for relaxation training. He suggests that EMG biofeedback training can be administered in the clinic while autogenic therapy procedures may be practiced at home as a maintenance of what has been learned in the clinic.

Studies have investigated the use of biofeedback to train individuals in acquiring the necessary relaxed state for systematic desensitization. Wickramasekera (cited in Gatchel and Price[50]) used this combination to successfully treat test anxiety. As a treatment approach to migraine headache, Sargent, et al.[69] combined finger temperature feedback with autogenic therapy procedures. Autogenic therapy was used to facilitate the biofeedback since both involved increasing the warmth of a target area, in this case the hands. The subjects experienced an improvement of $29 - 81\%$.

All of the therapeutic approaches described in the chapter, when correctly administered, are antagonistic to the physiological effects of stress. Regardless of the nature of the various methodologies, similar physiological effects take place. The use of one technique over another may be based on its compatibility with a particular patient. For instance, some patients will have very active and lucid imaginations and therefore can respond to the procedures inherent in imagery and autogenic therapy. Conversely, other individuals may display less of a tendency to feel comfortable with images or maintain a negative belief system. Therefore, these patients may achieve greater productivity (at least initially) with a more concrete method such as progressive muscle relaxation or biofeedback. In either case, Morse, et al. and Shapiro (both cited in Doleys, Meredith and Ciminero[70]) conclude that there is little difference in physiological and psychological effects among the successful practice of meditation, hypnosis and other relaxation methods. Ultimately, these methods commonly provide the ability to learn an antistress response which they may use to help control its psychosomatic effects.

IV PHYSIOLOGICAL RESPONSE TO MUSIC

Music has been a self-management tool in either an implicit or explicit fashion throughout its existence. As an art it is to be enjoyed for its aesthetic and entertainment value. But history repeatedly describes how mankind has (and certainly still does) use and even exploit the effects of music to nonaesthetic or nonentertainment ends. It is integral to social, business, educational and religious functioning. It pervades all aspects of daily life. Probably the most intriguing use of music is its application to all aspects of the health care and maintenance of the individual. From this connection, of course, grew the discipline of music therapy. Of the many applications of music as therapy, prior to or after its establishment as an organized discipline, its use as a facilitator for relaxation has been one of the most popular.

Obviously, a degree in music therapy is not necessary in order to use music to facilitate relaxation. Across all strata of society, it is probably used more for this purpose than any other noninvasive stimulus. However, addressing the questions of how and why specific types of music (relative to the individual) create these effects is necessary if we are going to continue to broaden its application as a therapeutic agent. To accomplish this, it is insufficient to remain in the subjective/abstract domain in which all arts exist. Objectively investigating the cause-and-effect relationships between physical/acoustical events in time and space and their effect on the social, intellectual, physiological and psychological response of the human being would appear to be the most productive direction of study. This section will examine the psychological and physiological response systems to music with particular attention given to its application as a relaxation agent. Hanser[71] notes that there are abundant inconsistencies in the literature concerning music and physiological response. Measurement involving the arts is quite elusive. The inherent emotional content and subsequent reaction to an art stimulus is very personal, very individual. Therefore, one must proceed with caution, accounting for every variable no matter how small or seemingly insignificant at the time, and in the course of study, avoid making hasty, inductive conclusions.

Music, like all sound, is transmitted through the air via oscillating waves of varying degrees of complexity. These waves carry much organized musical information such as pitch, intensity, timbre, harmony, tempo, rhythm – the combinations are limitless. Simply look at the multitude of compositions in all of music to date with no end in sight. Detection, interpretation and reaction are the intent of these compositions requiring operations of the ear and subsequent processing by the brain. The reader is referred to Hodges,[72] Roederer[73] and Critchley and Henson[74] for more specific information on the ear and brain with respect to normal hearing and cortical processing operations.

Music as an agent for relaxation and relaxation training must be examined on two levels, physiological and psychological. As noted earlier, there is substantial emotional involvement as an individual is exposed to stress. This involvement constitutes activity in the limbic system of the brain that, in excess, has negative effects on psychophysiological well-being. A primary and inherent property of music is that is elicits emotion, thereby also activating the limbic system. The use of music to exercise positive emotions either created by relaxation or accompanied by it could therefore very well be antagonistic to the effects of stress.

At this point, a description of brain function in response to a music stimulus for the purpose of relaxation is necessary for comparative study of the neurological response to stress. Levinthal[21] describes the major structures of the auditory pathway:

> " • the receptors of the cochlea of the ear,
> • the cochlear nucleus of the medulla,
> • olivary complex of the medulla,
> • the lateral lemniscus of the pons,
> • the medial geniculate nucleus of the thalamus,
> • an area of the temporal lobe of the neocortex." (p. 208)

The nerve connecting the cochlear mechanism and the medulla is the VIII cranial nerve or vestibulocochlear nerve which terminates at the cochlear nuclei of the dorsal medulla.[75] The medulla is the lowest structure of the brain stem and is also responsible for many autonomic functions including heart and respiration rate. Interestingly, impulses from the carotid sinus and aortic arch reach the medulla via the glossopharyngeal (IX) and Vagus (X) nerves respectively terminating at sites also located at the dorsal medulla. Parasympathetic control of the heart is also communicated via the vagus nerve.[76] McCleary and Moore[24] add that all sensory systems feed into the ascending reticular formation which ultimately maintains a proper level of electrical activity in most of the higher brain center. Ascending from the brain stem, it makes connections at midbrain formations of the thalamus and lateral hypothalamus. The thalamus diffuses the information throughout the neocortex while the hypothalamus feeds information directly into formations of the limbic system, particularly the septum and hippocampus. Blinkov and Glezer[77] add that the medial geniculate body is the most important relay nucleus in the auditory system. It is the thalamus auditory analyzer.[78]

In this somewhat simplified description of brain activity in response to auditory stimuli, amplification of three areas must be made in connection with the processing of music stimuli — the medulla, medial geniculate body and the hypothalamus. The preceding description pertained to the processing of nonmusic sound. However, the question must be raised at this point: What constitutes the difference between everyday sounds such as speech, noise, environmental sounds and music?

While investigating the subcortical processing of music stimuli, Scartelli[79] proposed that all nonmusical sounds contain almost all of the properties of music: pitch, timbre, harmony (dissonant and consonant) and intensity. The separating element, however, is the absence of an organized rhythm or pulse. Gabrielsson[80] tells us the rhythmic responses are psychological/physiological phenomena while sound sequences are acoustical/physical phenomena. The rhythmic response has three components:

- experiential-perceptual, cognitive and emotional variables that are rapid, dancing, complex and aggressive,
- behavioral-overt movements like tapping the foot and swaying the body,
- physiological-changes in respiration, heart rate, muscle tension, etc.

All of these activities occur simultaneously, with many different levels of interrelations and overlapping. Clynes and Walker[81] continue, stating "different pulse forms affect the state of the subject differently. The subtlety of form may give rise to peaceful or energetic, joyful or sexually exciting, enthusiastic or placid, and many shades in between. Because of its repetition its effect is hierarchically on a different level than other meaningful structures of music. It represents a frame of reference around which the music is built ... The form of the beat is the most obvious and primary repetitive phenomenon that music has to offer." (p. 191) Pulse repetition causes diminution of interest opening the door for other musical elements to take the forefront of attention, but remaining within the context of the pulse of beat or rhythm. "Each sound pulse form has its own qualitative character, and in its repetition becomes an attitude, which may have feeling or emotional significance." (p. 212-213)

Additionally, Scartelli[79] points out that the very first brain structure to receive auditory input is the medulla, the portion of the brain stem that controls autonomic function including the heart rate and respiration, our most vital and continuous rhythms or pulses. He hypothesized that auditory information that is accompanied or formatted within a rhythmic structure sends this signal to the higher centers of the auditory pathway in a different manner than nonrhythmical stimuli, perhaps with greater intensity. Wertheim[82] adds that rhythm has the capability to invigorate or sedate the listener, almost lulling him/her to sleep. Clynes and Walker[81] also note that repeated patterns can have a hypnotic effect where the rhythm takes us over. While little attention need be given to rate and shape of repetitive rhythms in music, both are elements of an attitude that persists throughout repetition. Wertheim continues, "How can such a complex influence be understood? Perhaps our present knowledge about the reticular system could provide the beginnings of an answer. We know that this particular area of the brain stem is concerned with a regulation of cortical electrical rhythms. We also know that there are abundant connections between the reticular formation and the auditory pathways. It may be that the rhythmical component of the auditory input has an impact on the whole cerebral cortex and also on large subcortical areas, via the extensive connection of the reticular formation with all of these regions." (p. 293) This charged information reaches the medial geniculate body housed in the thalamus by way of the ascending reticular formation which now activates the limbic system and cortex. Roederer[83] reinforces by reporting that physiologically, music elicits emotional responses in humans through interplay between the cortex and limbic system with the hypothalamus as mediator. He continues by citing that the limbic system, unlike the cortex, does not process and encode information. It is prewired at birth but continually communicates with and reacts to cortical activity. Since the brain stem is prewired or preprogrammed, and does not change as a result of input, rhythmic stimuli (music) would therefore exert its effect regardless of cortical content and input. This may explain (on a physiological level) the universal attraction that music has for human beings, regardless of training, culture or background.[79]

The role of the hypothalamus in stress and in music is amplified by Rider, et al.[84] reminding us that it is the initiator of the autonomic responses to stress. Additionally, the effects of music/imagery lie in the fact that the hypothalamus also has strong connections to the limbic system. They cite Achterberg's and Lawlis'[85] description of the fronto-limbic system which is the center of emotional control, image storage, motor control and memory storage. "The connection between music, guided imagery and progressive muscle relaxation and health is very likely a mechanism involving a (neural) hypothalamic-frontolimbic loop and a (neuroendocrine) hypothalamic-immunologic loop." (p. 48-49)

This myriad of subcortical activity eventually sends the information to the cortex or thinking area of the brain. In deference to the "right-brain" literature of the past fifteen years, a recent trend of research in indicating that both hemispheres are activated by musical stimuli in varying degrees and intensity. Jausovec[86] found that highly creative children showed a greater inter-hemisphericity than low creative children during artistic and nonartistic tasks as measured by EEG activity. In support, Konovalov and Otmakhova[87] found that during voluntary memorization, verbal information processing is carried out primarily in the left hemisphere, whereas musical analysis affects both hemispheres at about equal levels. They also used EEG activity as the dependent variable. Levy[88] notes that there is no evidence that creativity is an exclusive property of the right hemisphere. Real creativity almost certainly depends on the cooperation and communication between hemispheres. With particular respect to music, he adds that research shows that professional musicians could discriminate chords with equal proficiency in both hemispheres. In addition, he cites that people with high musical aptitude also showed more equal functioning between the two hemispheres.

If indeed, there is increased symmetrical activation of the brain during musical processing, the listener's thought processes would combine the characteristics of the hemispheres: analytical, logical, sequential and verbal in the dominant hemisphere and holistic, imaging, synthetic, spatial, nonverbal in the nondominant hemisphere. Wilson[89] cautions that the understanding of hemispheric specialization among those in the creative arts, has been, in some instances, taken too literally, going with the impression that we possess two autonomous brains. In the normal brain, this is physiologically impossible.

The two hemispheres are elegantly connected by a bundle of 200 million nerves called the corpus collosum, allowing constant communication between the right and left sides of the brain. Levy[88] supports this line of thought, adding that the two-brain myth was founded on an erroneous premise: if each hemisphere were specialized, each must function independently. In reality, the hemispheres integrate the specializations. It is that integration that gives rise to behavioral and mental processes that are greater than and different from each hemisphere's speciality.

As the hypothalamus and thalamus receive messages from the external environment via the senses, they are also fed information back down from various cortical structures. With more areas of the cortex activated by musical stimuli, there exists a reciprocal action feeding greater volumes of information back to the thalamic structures. Hence, amplification of activity in hypothalamus and thalamus. These structures, therefore, react stimulating autonomic and somatic response that we perceive as physical (affective) and emotional reactions. Regelski[90] notes that the lower brain regions communicate with both hemispheres, but the principle relationship the old brain (subcortical) has with the new (cortical) seems to be through the right hemisphere, particularly through the normalized activities of cognitive appraisal and subception that are very similar in type and function to those of the old brain. Through increased subcortical activity, particularly emotion, situational arousal states, motivational impulses and other kinds of nonverbal actions, significant learning takes place.

Common sense tells us that this finding is true. Whenever one is emotionally involved or vested in a learning experience, cortical activity (thinking) becomes more efficient. This cortical activity plays an important role in relaxation through the mechanisms of imagery and control of somatic function. Therefore, we may at this point hypothesize that the appropriate music stimuli might reinforce and enhance this mechanism. Landreth and Landreth[91] demonstrated that music produces induced heart rate changes in subjects, both increasing and decreasing. They noted that the effects tended to be greater with an increased knowledge of the music, i.e., greater cortical involvement.

More recently, investigations are beginning to concentrate on the chemical processes of the brain, specifically the location and activity of the opiate peptides (endorphines). It is now believed that the "high" received from activities such as long distance running, physical exertion, and even music may integrally involve endorphine secretion. Research has discovered the existence of specific opiate receptors in the brain and of endogenous (generated from within) peptides that interact with them. This information is having far-reaching consequences on the knowledge of pain mechanisms, affective disorders, and narcotic addiction. Goldstein[92] notes that opiate receptors not only mediate analgesic mechanisms, but also alter effect which may create an emotional detachment from the experience of suffering. Endorphins may "play some central role in the control of affective states ... known to be associated with limbic system function." (p. 1085)

In relating this information to musical reaction, Goldstein[93] found through survey, that music was determined to be one of the highest elicitors of thrills. He subsequently measured the effects that naloxone (an opiate antagonist) had on the thrill response to music. Naloxone did attenuate the response in varying degrees (highly significant in some subjects). In the course of the study, Goldstein came to the following conclusions: particular types of music relative to the individual are a very effective elicitor of the thrill response; perceived thrill was generally first felt in the spine, upper spine and neck and then spread to more peripheral regions of the body; and that this spreading was probably due to electrical activity in some brain areas with somatotopic organization (effects to the body), and with neural links to the limbic system and to central autonomic regulation. The amygdala (in the limbic system) is a possible candidate because it plays a principal role in emotional functions, autonomic discharge and discrimination of sensory modalities.[94] Therefore, emotional response involving the autonomic nervous system may be mediated by endorphins because of ties to the limbic system and resulting euphoria-like effects.

Therefore, as Roederer[83] states, there are a number of possible reasons why music retains its emotional appeal:

" • early training and exposure to certain types of music,
  • association of music with nature's sound environment,
  • associative recall of an emotional state felt during first exposure to a given piece,
  • the survival value connected with musical forms that provides a tendency for masses to congregate and uniformly behave. But mostly, it appears to be the activation of limbic function by the abstract sound of the music." (p. 43)

V MUSIC IN RELAXATION – STRESS REDUCTION

Hanser[71] tells us that the results of studies investigating the relaxation effects of music have lacked consistency. Alley[95] compared four conditions to determine what effects music had on relaxation training with heart rate and verbal reports acting as dependent variables. Results indicated that there was no difference among the music alone, verbal suggestions alone, music and verbal suggestion and contact-control group conditions. Sime and DeGood[96] compared EMG biofeedback training, progressive muscle relaxation training, and a placebo condition using music as a relaxation agent to determine what groups would most efficiently reduce frontalis muscle tension. No significant difference was achieved in the placebo/music group while the EMG biofeedback and progressive muscle relaxation training groups showed significant decreases in EMG activity. Barnes[97] found similarly poor effects of music on relaxation training conditions. When music was added to the relaxation training, results declined leading the experimenter to conclude that music was destabilizing and did not enhance recall ability (the dependent variable) when compared to relaxation only. (Note that music is referred to in these studies in broad terms giving little recognition of specific elements and their effects.)

In disagreement with these findings, Stoudenmire[98] found that music did not interfere with the relaxation process. Both progressive muscle relaxation and music conditions produced significant decreases in state anxiety. Peretti[99] reported significant reduction of anxiety in the presence of music variables. Calmness and contentment were reported when music was heard during a tension-producing task. These reports were corroborated by decreases in galvanic skin response. The author notes that people are accustomed to auditory and visual stimulation in their environment. The lack of background music (auditory deprivation) could easily lead to an increased anxiety level. These results agree with an earlier study by Peretti and Swenson[100] where they also found music to enhance the relaxation response as measured by galvanic skin response.

Using the Largo from Dvorak's *New World Symphony* and Sibelius' *The Swan of Tuonela*, Rohner and Miller[101] observed calming trends with subjects diagnosed as high state anxiety individual. Chetta[102] also reports successful application of music to desensitize and decrease preoperative anxiety in children. McFarland[103] compared the effects of two selections from Holst's *The Planets*: "Mars" (arousing and negative emotive) and "Venus" (calm and positive emotive). He observed that "Mars" terminated skin temperature increases and caused skin temperature decreases (conducive to stress) while "Venus" produced the opposite effect, conducive to relaxation. These data were corroborated by information yielded by the Affective Level Questionnaire. He concluded that music is a most powerful emotional stimulus creating physiological change.

VI COMBINATIONS OF MUSIC WITH OTHER RELAXATION TRAINING METHODS

Music, under the appropriate conditions, can facilitate changes in emotions, moods, and physiological states. As stated earlier, it can be a powerful agent by itself in producing a relaxation response. Given this fact, many researchers have conducted investigations to determine if particular types of music could be added to or incorporated with existing methods of relaxation such as progressive muscle relaxation, imagery and biofeedback to possibly produce a hybrid combination of methods that enhance and increase the efficiency of the relaxation training process.

One of the most well-known combinations in music therapy is Guided Imagery and Music. This method uses music as a catalyst to achieve altered states of consciousness. When properly presented, it predictably leads the listener from states of relaxation to intense emotional experiences. The choice of music is the major ingredient determining the resulting physical and emotional states. Bonny[104] contends that movement in music with its rise and fall of dynamics, brings about wide sweeps of levels or layers of consciousness. For greater detail, the reader is referred to Bonny and Savery.[105]

Using guided imagery and music to induce a rise in skin temperature, an indicator of parasympathetic nervous system activity, Peach[106] observed a mean increase of 5.4 degrees with short-term psychiatric patients, staff and students. This was accompanied by an appreciable gain on a relaxation perception scale.

Rider, Floyd and Kirkpatrick[84] state that music, imagery and progressive muscle relaxation may be effective. They found that decreases of circadian amplitude and entrainment of corticosteroid and temperature rhythms were significant during music listening by adult nurses with sleep disturbances due to inconsistent working shifts.

There appears to be a synthesis and possibly symbiotic relationship between music and imagery. In comparing the effects of music to relaxation on the production of visual imagery, Quittner and Glueckauf[107] showed that imagery production of their subjects was significantly higher under the music condition than under either the relaxation or control condition. Rider[108] suggests that imagery helps music in pain reduction and biofeedback effectiveness in relaxation. "The entrained music/imagery condition suggested that autonomic responses behave similarly to voluntary muscle responses, either through entrainment of neural pain impulses by sensory signals in the thalamus or through recurrent inhibition of the endoloxonergic system, the inhibitory division of the endorphinergic system." (p. 190) As Peach[106] notes, "enough evidence now exists to conclude that music is a reliable vehicle for image productions." (p. 28)

A number of researchers investigated the effects of combining music with progressive muscle relaxation training. Kibler and Rider[109] showed that music paired with progressive muscle relaxation produced greater increases in finger temperature (an indicator of relaxation) than did music alone or progressive muscle relaxation training alone, although the difference was not statistically significant. However, all three conditions experienced significant increases in mean finger temperature. Wager[110] recently obtained promising results by combining imagery, progressive muscle relaxation and music

(Halpern's *Spectrum Suite*) to reduce heart and respiration rates (sympathetic nervous system activity) of patients with chronic obstructive pulmonary disease.

VII MUSIC AND BIOFEEDBACK

As previously discussed, both biofeedback and music, on their own, have been successfully used as facilitators of relaxation training. It was inevitable that the two be combined in an attempt to observe the effects that one technique might have on the other. The small amount of research to date suggests a number of theories on why music might increase the efficiency and effects of biofeedback-assisted relaxation training.

The auditory feedback of most biofeedback instruments is in the form of clicks or tones. After an extended period of time, however, this feedback becomes monotonous and possibly irritating. The clicking is basically a form of punishment telling the patient that (s)he is not meeting the desired physiological level and, therefore, the adversive sound is present. However, behavioral principles state that punishment procedures should be used only when positive measures have failed. With that in mind, one of the earlier applications of music to biofeedback was the use of music as a reinforcement for achieving a target level of relaxation. In essence, silence or the elimination of the auditory feedback has been the reinforcement or reward (technically a removal of an adversive stimulus). Music, on the other hand, may replace the silence as an effective reward for many patients and, in doing so, may also relieve boredom in the session and increase motivation to improve.

An illustration of this combination of music and biofeedback can be seen in Wolfe.[111] Cerebral palsied individuals were reinforced with music when they righted their heads (by their own control) to the limits of acceptable angles which were set on a mercury switch by the therapist. The switch was located on a headband and terminated the music if the child's head tilted too far to either side. In this quite pure display of behavioral strategy, the control of the head could be slowly increased (shaped) by decreasing the angle limits of the switch to receive the reinforcement of music. In spite of many contaminating factors reported by Wolfe, this procedure yielded reasonable results.

Using contingent music for achieved low EMG biofeedback levels to reduce tension headache, Epstein, Hersen and Hemphill[112] found that, in all sessions, music feedback decreased microvolt activity of the frontalis area. No difference was reported when using the standard feedback. It was additionally noted that headache pain increased when the music feedback was terminated in this single case study report. Obviously, for music to be reinforcing, it must agree with the preference, taste and background of the subject. Determination is most easily achieved by simply asking the subject what (s)he likes. This topic will be discussed in greater detail later in this section.

The second format of combining music and biofeedback is the use of music in a noncontingent manner or as a primary stimulus for fostering and training relaxation. This design has shown some promising results with relatively simple and accessible application in clinical settings.

Scartelli[113] used popular instrumental music that, by definition[114] could be classified as sedative to assist the biofeedback relaxation training of the extensor muscle on the more afflicted arm of spastic cerebral palsied young adults. Compared to a contact-control group who received biofeedback training, the music/biofeedback group achieved a reduction of extensor (forearm) tension of 65% versus 32.5% in the biofeedback-only group over a five week training period. In addition, those subjects in the biofeedback/music group consistently reported greater feeling of overall relaxation when compared to the biofeedback-only group.

Using a similar design, but adding a music-only group, Scartelli[115] obtained similar results measuring frontalis activity of normal-tensive adults. Using classical instrumental music, the music-biofeedback group experienced the greatest decrease of microvolt levels ($p<.001$) with the music-only group following ($p<.01$). The biofeedback-only group displayed a decrease, although not significant. These results do not necessarily imply that music or music-biofeedback are better than biofeedback alone, rather it might be concluded that they were more efficient within the time afforded in training. The trend of data within the biofeedback-only group suggested that, given more time, this group would have also achieved significant decreases.

In both of these studies, music was added to the relaxation training environment after the subjects were trained to properly use the biofeedback instrumentation. The role of the music was as background or ambient sound in an effort to use its hypothesized effects to enhance the EMG biofeedback-assisted relaxation training. However, the investigator observed confusion in many of the subjects training under the music-biofeedback conditions. These individuals reported experiencing doubt as to what auditory stimulus to attend. Some chose to primarily listen to the music and periodically check themselves against the biofeedback auditory response. The others primarily attended to the clicking of the biofeedback instrument while attempting to use the music as ambient background. Both situations were apparently successful upon examination of the data. However, concern arose over the mental energy that must obviously be expended to deal with the two stimuli simultaneously, particularly when the goal of the procedure was relaxation. This concern led to a third investigation[116] which compared simultaneous versus sequenced administration of the two treatment variables of EMG biofeedback and music. The results of the study, using normal-tensive adults, clearly favored a sequenced treatment design, either music preceding biofeedback of vice versa over the simultaneous administration seen in the previous studies. It should be noted at this point that all three groups achieved reduced tension levels of the frontalis muscle. Subjects in the sequenced conditions, almost unanimously reported the music as being very comforting and conducive to satisfying rest. An additional result of the study showed the possibilities of transferring the relaxation gained through the biofeedback training to music listening while maintaining the relaxed state. Remember that the ultimate goal of the biofeedback-assisted relaxation training is to fade dependency on the biofeedback instrument while maintaining the learned ability to relax. Music could easily be utilized as a cue or stimulus for maintaining the relaxation skills learned through biofeedback training. A long-term study would be required to test this assumption.

Reynolds[117] added an autogenic therapy procedure to EMG biofeedback-assisted relaxation of the frontalis with background music and concluded that this combination was more effective than music-biofeedback and a control condition. He noted that "combining EMG auditory feedback with other treatment procedures enhanced the benefits gained from using EMG auditory feedback alone." (p. 175)

There are several possible theories to be discussed with respect to why music might improve the effect and efficiency of biofeedback-assisted relaxation training. The most obvious is that music, in and of itself, is pleasurable and therefore contains inherent reinforcing properties. It also blocks extraneous sounds that might interfere with concentration and relaxation. Curiously, some of the sounds masked by the music stimulus are body sounds such as stomach rumbles, belches, etc., that are a source of embarrassment and almost always followed by tension caused by attempts to suppress these sounds.

In general, appropriately chosen music is a comforting alternative to silence or the biofeedback auditory feedback. Additionally, silence itself can be adversive. We live in a very stimulating environment that includes a constant bombardment of sounds. As is human nature, we acclimate and adjust to this stimulation thus becoming accustomed to its almost constant presence. The reader may recall that Adler and Adler[60] target intruding images and thoughts as damaging to the relaxation process. Music can be used to prevent vacillation of concentration by helping the subject cue in on appropriate thoughts and images germane to the relaxation training and ultimately block out these intruding thoughts. The Guided Imagery and Music technique serves as an appropriate prototype. Adler and Adler also expressed that patients almost always use images to evoke the memory of the sensation of relaxation. Music can be used as an external device to help cue that memory and enhance the imagery process.

In terms of neurological function, the following deductive sequence of research findings can help illustrate how music could help maintain a relaxed state and block out intruding, tension-producing thoughts. The Russian neurologist Luria[118] found that the nondominant hemisphere is directly concerned with analysis of information from the body. Keep in mind that the nondominant hemisphere experiences increased activity in response to music stimuli.[70][119] Budzynski[120] adds that decreased critical, analytical, logical and linear thought decreases physical arousal. These functions all primarily take place in the dominant cerebral hemisphere. He also makes a strong case for recognizing the importance of nondominant hemisphere control of somatic functions.[121] To complete this argument, Patterson[122] deduced that nondominant hemisphere activity can 'block' dominant activity resulting in a more efficient relaxation response. Based on these deduced findings, one could conclude that music can be used as a suppressant of certain dominant hemisphere functions resulting in a more active communication between the brain and body with respect to deliberate relaxation. The author has found that instrumental music is highly preferable to vocal music, thus avoiding lyrics that may require language processing — a primarily dominant hemispheric activity.

VIII CHOOSING MUSIC FOR RELAXATION

At this point, we must examine the inevitable question – What types of music are best for use in relaxation training procedures? Should it be sedative, slightly stimulative, classical, popular, on and on. Because of the extraordinarily broad range of individual experiences with music, it appears veritably impossible to arrive at one specific type of music that would yield a consistent sedative response. Research directed in this area is difficult but necessary in spite of the apparent futility of the task. As a start, Standley[123] suggests that much of the benefit of music's effects depends on the individual patient's music preference. Hodges,[72] Farnsworth,[124] Deutsch,[125] and Radocy and Boyle[126] discuss the nature, background and theory of music preference and taste. With an understanding of this material, one might conclude that familiar music or music that agrees with the developed taste and preferences of the patient may very well result in more efficient and predictable effects. This does not necessarily mean that a person who has a strong preference for rock and roll must use it exclusively to learn relaxation. However, if that same person has virtually little or no experience with classical (serious) music, a selection from that genre may create counterproductive effects, even if it could be broadly defined, in a consensus manner, as sedative. As a therapist, one must keep in mind that it is basic human nature to reject that which is unfamiliar to us. The greater the disturbance of the patient, the more profound this rejection.

In recent years, the research literature has included reports discussing the effects of specific types of music, particularly sedative versus stimulative. Hanser[71] reinforces that there is a problem with the operational understanding of music classified as sedative and music classified as stimulative along with their respective projected effects on the listener. Hodges[72] is in support, adding that a review of available data clearly supports the hypothesis that listening to music clearly does influence physiological response. However, the literature remains unclear with regard to defining stimulative and sedative music with present understanding being too general for useful purposes in the clinic. More specifically, Harrer and Harrer[127] state that autonomic response depends on:

- reactivity of the autonomic regulatory processes which are influenced by age, sex, mode of life physical fitness, state of health and temporary factors like fatigue and diet,
- emotional reactivity,
- attitude toward music's importance in one's life, and immediate attitude toward the piece of music presented in the test situation.

As a result of the ambiguity involved in defining stimulative and sedative music, a number of studies have been conducted in an effort to improve understanding and possibly change the direction or perspective of future research. Taylor[128] in questioning the accuracy of pre-categorized stimulative and sedative music, found that people react to music in a highly individualized manner, and pre-categorized music, in fact, may very well not elicit its intended effects. Through experimental design, Borling[129] agrees with Taylor by revealing that statistical comparisons of sedative and stimulative music conditions for alpha production showed no significant difference from one another.

Stratton and Zalinowski[130] found no one particular type of music more effective than any other in relaxation training (except for atonal). There were even no differences between music labeled as soothing or stimulating. Of note, the subjects in this investigation varied in degree of relaxation with the single most important factor being the liking for the music. They suggest that the subject should be allowed to choose the kind of music most appealing to them for relaxation. Indeed, Smith and Morris[131] showed that liking for the music positively correlated with performance, expectancy, and concentration.

The advantages of using subject-preferred music in the delivery room was illustrated in a study conducted by Hanser, Larson and O'Connell[132] in which it was determined that enhanced concentration and reduced sensation of pain were reported by 100% of the subjects during labor. The investigators emphasized positive associations with the music and using it as a diverter from the discomfort and hospital environment in their methodology.

The reader may recall in the Introduction a caution to observe all variables and their effects if possible. Music, itself, has a multitude of explicit variables (pitch, rhythm, harmony, melody, etc.) in their innumerable forms. It also has an infinite number of implicit variables such as the individual's relationship with music, his/her experiences (particularly emotional), tastes and preferences, etc. Combined, the researcher is presented with the formidable task of discovering the most appropriate and effective music or auditory stimulus to enhance relaxation. Add to this, the necessity to understand, as much as possible, the nature of psychophysiological and emotional reactions involved in stress and anxiety along with their counterparts of relaxation and control.

IX CONCLUSIONS AND DIRECTIONS FOR FUTURE INVESTIGATION

In spite of the frequency of success in applying biofeedback technology and/or music to relaxation training, it is important to note that neither is a panacea. Efficient relaxation requires an efficient learning process. Application of various intervention devices and methods are cues or aids in this learning process. All of the work is ultimately performed by the brain and reciprocal function of the body. The choice of a particular method or variable to train physical relaxation requires knowledge of a patient's intellectual, psychological/emotional, and physical states. Therefore, it is important to find initially the appropriate method or combination of methods for each individual. Once this determination is made, the training can be expected to proceed with maximum efficiency. With regard to biofeedback-assisted relaxation training, Page and Schaub[133] state that differences among personality types can result in considerably varying degrees of effectiveness within a given population.

In the previous chapter, we discussed the importance of identifying the most appropriate type or choice of music for a specific outcome with a particular individual. Through an investigation of the literature, it can be concluded that we must avoid pre-categorized sedative music for facilitating relaxation. Simply put, the effect of music is ultimately very individualized.

In addition to recognizing the problems of using pre-categorized music, the therapist must also be aware of the specific emotions elicited by the music for each patient. In many cases, it would be to the therapist's advantage to use music that is psychologically inert. Music that arouses memories, particularly negative can be counter-productive to the goal of relaxation. An informal inquiry of the patient should tell you if the music arouses feelings that are connected with a past experience. If so, it should be discarded. The piece should avoid such connections in order to establish an individual identity with relaxation guidance and cues – a musical mantra if you will. The market recognizes this fact with the popularity of "New Age Music," "Space Music," "Environmental Sounds," all of which are extremely popular as effectors of relaxation and contemplation.

As caution must be used in the choice of music in relaxation training, it must be equally exercised in the application of biofeedback. Early enthusiasm over biofeedback has largely passed and is currently undergoing evaluation and re-evaluation of its techniques, possibilities, and limitations.

Criticisms that have surfaced regard the problems of inadequate testing and experimentation, small sample groups or case-study reports and ambiguous understanding of what biofeedback can and cannot do. These critics feel that many of the claims made in the biofeedback literature are, at least for the present, ambitious until validated by research that attends to the problems listed above.

One example of these problems is the assumption that there is an inherent power within the biofeedback instrument[134] that will cause a change in the patient who has taken a passive role in treatment, much like taking a prescribed drug. This effect is termed "the ghost in the box." The authors continue by cautioning: "the biofeedback instrument ... is no more and no less than a mirror ... Like a mirror, the biofeedback instrument has no inherent power to create change; it merely feeds back information." (p. 1004) Therefore, the patient can only take this mirrored information from the instrument and use it to change him/herself through his/her own intellectual, cognitive, psychological and physiological control mechanisms. Learning to relax is a skill and, like any other skill, it must be practiced on a conscientious and regular basis to be mastered.

Therefore, when one attempts to use biofeedback and music in relaxation training, one must recognize the applications and limitations of both variables separately and in combination. Both music and biofeedback, individually, have been shown to be effective tools in stress management and relaxation training. However, in light of criticism, future work involving both variables must be extremely careful not to muddy the water. Research must avoid relying heavily on subjective and descriptive reports regarding patient response and sensation resulting from exposure to the music. Objective, physiological measurement must first be taken, the data scrutinized, and significant trends and consistent cause-and-effect relationships between the independent variables of music and biofeedback and the objective (physiological) dependent variables must be identified. Once consistencies can be established on these objective levels, we can then afford to venture out into the less tangible emotional/psychological domains as the dependent variable.

It would benefit those who may be interested in further pursuing information concerning behavior and physiology to become more familiar with the principles and findings of such areas as behavioral medicine psychology, psychosomatic medicine and psychophysiology. With an increased awareness of these disciplines, we will expand our knowledge of not only psychological, behavioral and physical (somatic) activity, but also neurological and endocrinological as well. Subsequently we may take this information and apply it to human interaction with, and in response to, music. Indeed, the nature of behavior may very well be explained with greater knowledge and understanding of these systems and their interactions.

Future research should not limit itself to organized music as the auditory stimuli. Stimuli including white noise, environmental sounds, synthesizer and computer generated music must all undergo continued and extensive investigation for their effects. Additionally, specific elements of traditional music must be scrutinized for their respective effects. The research must determine such factors as the placement of the music or auditory stimulus in treatment, its intensity, genre, and most efficient combination with other treatment avenues.

Finally, it is important to maintain sense of direction with respect to where research and clinical application are going in both music and biofeedback in relaxation training and other self-management training procedures. In essence, this direction lies in teaching, increasing, and maintaining patient efficacy thus increasing control of the physiological state via psychological, cognitive, and behavioral intervention. Albert Bandura, who pioneered this approach, tells us that we must increase our awareness of how one's beliefs can affect the course of an illness and subsequent recovery.[135] In support, Weinman[136] using EMG biofeedback-assisted relaxation training to significantly reduce states of anxiety, depression, and tension symptoms of high-stress individuals, concluded that this sample attributed improvement to the belief that they were increasing the control of their minds and bodies.

Maximizing self-control should, therefore, be our goal with disorders ranging from simple tension headache to the treatment of cancer. Music and biofeedback have individually and, to a small extent, in combination with one another, been applied successfully to these ends. Certainly, with the increasing strides in medical and computer technologies the upcoming years will yield exciting advances and applications in this area by those who proceed with caution, open eyes, and open minds.

GLOSSARY

Afferent – information or impulses emanating from the periphery and travelling to the center.

Amygdala – group of nerve cells within the limbic lobe of the brain responsible for controlling motor responses associated with feeding. It is considered a portion of the "emotional brain."[137]

Catecholamine – a classification of neurotransmitters that can alter nervous system and metabolic function. Epinephrine and norepinephrine are the most common of the catecholamines.

Corticosteroid – a stress-activated steroid hormone produced by the adrenal gland. This family of steroids includes corticosterone, cortisol and cortisone all having profound effects on metabolic and immune responses.

Efferent – information or impulses emanating from the center and travelling out to the periphery.

Endorphin – a peptide that acts as an endogenous opiate.

Enkephalin – a group of opiate peptides that can act as neurotransmitters.

Epinephrine – (adrenaline) a hormone produced by the adrenal medulla, endogenously activated by sympathetic nervous system stimulation and effects metabolic function.

Glossopharyngeal Nerve – the ninth cranial nerve that primarily carries sensory (taste and visceral) and motor information to the brain.

Hippocampus – a portion of the limbic system thought to be involved with alertness and avoidance behavior.

Homeostasis – state of balance or equilibrium.

Limbic system – group of structures inferior to the cortex responsible for emotional, autonomic and memory function.[137]

Lymphocyte – white blood corpuscle responsible for defending against disease-causing substances in the body.

Medial Geniculate Nucleus – the auditory analyzer located near the thalamus and acts as a "dispatcher" to auditory cortical areas

Neurotransmitter – a chemical substance released into the synaptic cleft that will either inhibit or promote electrochemical transfer of information from brain cell to brain cell.

Norepinephrine – (noradrenaline) a hormone produced by the adrenal medulla affecting blood pressure, muscular coordination and mood.[137]

Pituitary – endocrine gland located below the hypothalamus that ultimately stimulates endocrine organ function and secretion.

Proprioceptive – awareness of the position of and forces upon the body.

Reticular Formation – groups of cells and fibers that ascend and descend through the brain stem and mid brain. It is important in influencing states of alertness and reflexes and the amount of electrical activity to the cortex.

Transducer – change from one form of energy to another (mechanical to electrical for example).

Vagus Nerve – the tenth cranial nerve responsible for much motor and sensory function information to the brain.

Vestibularcochlear Nerve – the eighth cranial nerve, also known as the acoustic nerve.

Volition – exercising the will. (Example: will to control or change a particular body function.)

REFERENCES

Psychology Today = PT

1 Silver, M. & Blanchard, E.: Biofeedback and relaxation: Training in the treatment of psychophysiological disorders: Or are the machines really necessary? In: D. Shapiro, J. Stoyva, J. Kamiya, T. Barber, N. Miller & G. Schwartz (Eds.), *Biofeedback and Behavioral Medicine: 1979/1980*. New York: Aldine Publishing Co., 1981, pp. 109-131.

2 Shapiro, D.: Biofeedback and behavioral medicine. In: D. Shapiro, J. Stoyva, J. Kamiya, T. Barber, N. Miller & G. Schwartz (Eds.), *Biofeedback and Behavioral Medicine: 1979/1980*. New York: Aldine Publishing Co., 1981, pp. 3-13.

3 Spiegel, H. & Spiegel, D.: *Trance and Treatment: Clinical Uses of Hypnosis*. New York: Basic Books, 1978.

4 American Biotechnology Corporation: *Brainwave Training Manual for the A-3 EEG*. Ossining, NY: Author, 1979.

5 Astor, A.: An introduction to biofeedback. *American Journal of Orthopsychiatry*, 1977, **47**, pp. 615-625.

6 Rosenbaum, R.: The interview method of assessment of the coronary-prone behavior pattern. In: T. Dembroski, S. Wiess, J. Shields, S. Haynes & M. Feinleib (Eds.), *Coronary-Prone Behavior*. New York: Springer-Verlag, 1975, pp. 55-70.

7 Levi, L.: *Society, Stress, and Disease*. London: Oxford University Press, 1971.

8 Maier, S. & Laudenslagen, M.: Stress and health: Exploring the links. *Psychology Today*, August 1985, pp. 44-49.

9 Gatchel, R. & Baum, A.: *An Introduction to Health Psychology*. Reading, MA: Addison-Wesley, 1983.

10 Green, E., Green, A. & Walters, E.: Voluntary control of internal states: Psychological and physiological. *Journal of Transpersonal Psychology*, 1970, **1**, pp. 1-26.

11 Krupat, E.: A delicate imbalance. *PT*, November 1986, pp. 22-26.

12 Selye, H.: *The Stress of Life*. New York: McGraw-Hill, 1956.

13 Benson, H.: *The Relaxation Response*. New York: Avon Books, 1975.

14 Anderson, J.: Relaxation training and relaxation-related procedures. In: D. Doleys, R. Meredith & A Ciminero (Eds.), *Behavioral Medicine*. New York: Plenum Press, 1982, pp. 69-82.

15 Wolpe, J.: *Psychotherapy and Reciprocal Inhibition*. Stanford: Stanford University Press, 1958.

16 Curtis, G.: Psychosomatic and chronobiology: Possible implications of neuromuscular rhythms. *Psychosomatic Medicine*, 1972, **34**, pp. 235-256.

17 Asterita, M.: *The Physiology of Stress*. New York: Human Sciences Press, 1985.

18 Suinn, R.: *Fundamentals of Behavior Pathology*. New York: John Wiley & Sons, 1970.

19 Green, E. & Green, A.: General and specific applications of thermal biofeedback. In: J. Basmajian (Ed.), *Biofeedback: Principles and Practice for Clinicians*. Baltimore: Williams and Wilkins, 1983, pp. 211-277.

20 Weissburg, M.: *Dangerous Secrets: Maladaptive Responses to Stress*. (2nd ed.) New York: W.W. Norton, 1983.

21 Levinthal, C.: *Introduction to Physiological Psychology* (2nd ed). Englewood Cliffs, NJ: Prentice Hall, 1983.

22 Teylor, T.: An introduction to the neurosciences. In: M. Wittrock, J. Beatty, J. Bogen, M. Gazzaniga, H. Jerison, S. Krashen, R. Nebes & T. Teylor (Eds.), *The Human Brain*. Englewood Cliffs, NJ: Prentice Hall, 1977, pp. 3-38.

23 Leukel, F.: *Introduction to Physiological Psychology* (2nd ed.). St. Louis, MO: C.V. Mosby, Co., 1972.

24 McCleary, R. & Moore, R.: *Subcortical Mechanisms of Behavior*. New York: Basic Books, 1965.

25 Buck, R.: *Human Motivation of Emotion*. New York: Wiley, 1976.

26 Hilgard, E.: *The Experience of Hypnosis*. New York: Harcourt, Brace and World, Inc., 1968.

27 Adams, P.: *The New Self-Hypnosis*. Hollywood, CA: Wilshire Books, 1976.

28 Zilbergeld, B., Edelstien, M. & Aaroz, D. (Eds.): *Hypnosis: Questions and Answers*. New York: W.W. Horton, 1986.

29   Negley-Parker, E.: Physiological correlates and effects of hypnosis. In: B. Zilbergeld, M. Edelstien & D. Aaroz (Eds.), *Hypnosis: Questions and Answers*. New York: W.W. Horton, 1986, pp. 9-16.

30   Long, P.: Medical mesmerism. *PT*, January 1986, pp. 28-29.

31   Pratt, G.: Hypnosis and stress management. In: B. Zilbergeld, M. Edelstien & D. Aaroz (Eds.), *Hypnosis: Questions and Answers*. New York: W.W. Horton, 1986, pp. 320-324.

32   Peterfy, G.: Hypnosis. In: E. Wittkower & H. Warnes, (Eds.), *Psychosomatic Medicine: Its Clinical Applications*. Hagerstown, MD: Harper and Row, 1977, pp. 129-137.

33   Schultz, J. & Luthe, W.: *Autogenic Methods*. New York: Grune and Stratton, 1969.

34   Luthe, W. & Blumberger, S.: Autogenic therapy. In: E. Wittkower & H. Warnes, (Eds.), *Psychosomatic Medicine: Its Clinical Applications*. Hagerstown, MD: Harper and Row, 1977, pp. 146-165.

35   Jaffe, D. & Bressler, D.: Guided imagery: Healing through the mind's eye. In: J. Shorr, G. Sobel, P. Robin, & J. Connella (Eds.), *Imagery: Its Many Dimensions and Applications*. New York: Plenum Press, 1980, pp. 253-266.

36   Turk, D.: Cognitive learning approaches: Applications in health care. In: D. Doleys, R. Meredith & A. Ciminero (Eds.), *Behavioral Medicine*. New York: Plenum Press, 1982, pp. 45-68.

37   Norris, P.: Biofeedback, voluntary control, and human potential. *Biofeedback and Self-Regulation*, 1986, **11**, pp. 1-20.

38   Vattano, A.: Self-management procedures for coping with stress. *Social Work*, 1978, **23**, pp. 113-119.

39   Norvell.: *The Miracle Power of Transcendental Meditation*. New York: Barnes and Noble Books, 1972.

40   Bloomfield, A., Cain, M., Jaffe, D. & Kory, R.: *T.M.: Discovering Inner Energy and Overcoming Stress*. New York: Dell, 1975.

41   Bakel, D.: *Psychology of Medicine*. New York: Springer Publishing Co., 1979.

42   Jacobson, E.: *Progressive Relaxation*. Chicago: University of Chicago Press, 1929.

43   Bernstein, D. & Borkevec, T.: *Progressive Relaxation Training: A Manual for the Helping Professions*. Champaign, IL: Research Press, 1973.

44   Walker, E.: *Learn to Relax*. Englewood Cliffs, NJ: Prentice Hall, 1975.

45   Wachtel, P.: *Psychoanalysis and Behavior Therapy*. New York: Basic Books, 1977.

46   Wickramasekera, I.: *Biofeedback, Behavior Therapy, and Hypnosis*. Chicago: Nelson Hall, 1976.

47   Wolf, S.: Neurophysical factors in electromyographic feedback for neuromotor disturbances. In: J. Basmajian (Ed.), *Biofeedback: Principles and Practice for Clinicians* (2nd ed.). Baltimore: Williams and Wilkins, 1983, pp. 5-22.

48   Fuller, G.: Current status of biofeedback in clinical practice. *American Psychologist*, 1978, **33**, pp. 39-48.

49   Sargent, J.: Biofeedback and biocybernetics. In: E. Wittkower & H. Warnes (Eds.), *Psychosomatic Medicine*. Hagerstown, MD: Harper and Row, 1977, pp. 166-171.

50   Gatchel, R. & Price, K. (Eds.): *Clinical Applications of Biofeedback: Appraisal and Status*. New York: Pergamon Press, 1979.

51   Lubar, J.: Electroencephalographic biofeedback and neurological applications. In: J. Basmajian (Ed.), *Biofeedback: Principles and Practice for Clinicians* (2nd ed.). Baltimore: Williams and Wilkins, 1983, pp. 37-61.

52   Kuhlman, W. & Kaplan, B.: Clinical applications of EEG feedback training. In: R. Gatchel & K. Price (Eds.), *Clinical Applications of Biofeedback: Appraisal and Status*. New York: Pergamon Press, 1979, pp. 65-96.

53   Stoyva, J. & Kamiya, J.: Electrophysiological studies of dreaming as the prototype of a new strategy in the study of consciousness. *Psychological Review*, 1968, **75**, pp. 195-205.

54   Plotkin, W.: The alpha experience revisited: Biofeedback in the transformation of psychological state. In: D. Shapiro, J. Stoyva, J. Kamiya, T. Barber, N. Miller & G. Schwartz (Eds.), *Biofeedback and Behavioral Medicine: 1979/1980*. New York: Aldine Publishers, 1981, pp. 75-94.

55   Basmajian, J.: Electromyography comes of age. *Science*, 1972, **197**, pp. 603-609.

56   Kukulka, C. & Basmajian, J.: Assessment of an audio-visual feedback device used in motor training. *American Journal of Physical Medicine*, 1975, **54**, pp. 194-207.

57   Morris, A.: Biofeedback comes of age. *American Journal of Corrective Therapy*, 1976, **30**, p. 35.

58   Basmajian, J.: *Muscles Alive, 2nd Ed*. Baltimore: Williams and Wilkins, 1967.

59   Basmajian, J.: Electromyography: Single motor unit training. In: R. Thompson (Ed.), *Bioelectric Recording Techniques*. New York: Academic Press, 1974.

60   Adler, C. & Adler, S.: Biofeedback and psychosomatic disorders. In: J. Basmajian (Ed.), *Biofeedback: Principles and Practice for the Clinicians* (2nd ed.). Baltimore, MD: Williams and Wilkins, 1983, pp. 255-274.

61   Fridlund, A. & Cacioppo, J.: Guidelines for human electromyographic research. *Psychophysiology*, 1986, **23**, pp. 567-589.

62   Alexander, A. & Smith, D.: Clinical applications of biofeedback. In: R. Gatchel & K. Price (Eds.), *Clinical Applications of Biofeedback: Appraisal and Status*. New York: Pergamon Press, 1979, pp. 112-133.

63   Katkin, E. & Goldband, S.: The placebo effect and biofeedback. In: R. Gatchel & K. Price (Eds.), *Clinical Applications of Biofeedback: Appraisal and Status*. New York: Pergamon Press, 1979, pp. 173-186.

64   Lacy, J.: Regulatory physiology and biofeedback. In: L. White and B. Tursky (Eds.), *Clinical Biofeedback: Efficacy and Mechanisms*. New York: Guilford Press, 1982, pp. 411-421.

65   Sharpley, C. & Rogers, H.: A meta-analysis of frontalis EMG levels with biofeedback and alternative procedures. *Biofeedback and Self-Regulation*, 1984, **9**, pp. 385-394.

66   Blanchard, E., Jaccard, Z., Andrasik, R., Gvarnieri, P. & Jurish, S.: Reduction in headache patients' medical expenses associated with biofeedback and relaxation treatments. *Biofeedback and Self-Regulation*, 1985, **10**, pp. 63-68.

67   Stoyva, J.: Guidelines in cultivating general relaxation: Biofeedback and autogenic therapy combined. In: J. Basmajian (Ed.), *Biofeedback: Principles and Practice for the Clinicians* (2nd ed.). Baltimore, MD: Williams and Wilkins, 1983, pp. 149-169.

68   Patel, C. & North, W.: Randomized controlled trial of yoga and biofeedback in the management of hypertension. *Lancet*, 1975, **2**, pp. 93-95.

69   Sargent, J., Green, E. & Walters, E.: Preliminary report on the use of autogenic feedback techniques in the treatment of migraine and tension headaches. *Psychosomatic Medicine*, 1973, **35**, pp. 129-135.

70   Doleys, D., Meredith, R. & Ciminero, A.: *Behavioral Medicine*. New York: Plenum Press, 1982.

71   Hanser, S.: Music therapy and stress reduction research. *JMT*, 1985, **22**, pp. 193-206.

72   Hodges, D. (Ed.): *Handbook of Music Psychology*. Dubuque, IA: Kendall/Hunt, 1980.

73   Roederer, J.: *Introduction to the Physics and Psychophysics of Music*, 2nd ed. New York: Springer-Verlag, 1975.

74   Critchley, M. & Henson, R. (Eds.): *Music and the Brain*. London: Heinemann Medical Books, 1977.

75   Stratton, D.: *Neurophysiology*. New York: McGraw-Hill, 1981.

76   Schneiderman, N.: Animal models relating behavioral stress and cardiovascular pathology. In: T. Dembroski, S. Weiss, J. Shields, S. Haynes & M. Feinleib (Eds.), *Coronary-Prone Behavior*. New York: Springer-Verlag, 1978, pp. 155-182.

77   Blinkov, S. & Glezer, I.: *The Human Brain in Figures and Tables*. New York: Basic Books, 1968.

78   Moller, A.: *Auditory Physiology*. New York: Academic Press, 1983.

79   Scartelli, J.: *Neurophysiologic Paradigm of Selected Psychology of Arts Theories*. Paper presented at the meeting of the NAMT, Mid-Atlantic Region, Niagara Falls, NY, March, 1985.

80   Gabrielsson, A.: Perception and performance of musical rhythm. In: M. Clynes (Ed.), *Music, Mind, and Brain*. New York: Plenum Press, 1982, pp. 159-169.

81   Clynes, M. & Walker, J.: Neurobiologic functions of rhythm, time, and pulse in music. In: M. Clynes (Ed.), *Music, Mind, and Brain*. New York: Plenum Press, 1982, pp. 171-216.

82   Wertheim, N.: Is there an anatomical localization for music facilities? In: M. Critchley & R. Henson (Eds.), *Music and the Brain*. London: Heinemann Medical Books Limited, 1977, pp. 282-279.

83   Roederer, J.: Physical and neuropsychological foundations of music. In: M. Clynes (Ed.), *Music, Mind, and Brain*. New York: Plenum Press, 1982, pp. 37-46.

84   Rider, M., Floyd, J. & Kirkpatrick, J.: The effect of music, imagery, and relaxation on adrenal corticosteroids and the re-entrainment of circadian rhythms. *JMT*, 1985, **22**, pp. 46-58.

85   Achterberg, J. & Lawlis, G.: *Bridges of the Bodymind: Behavioral Approaches to Healthcare*. Champaign, IL: I.P.A.T., 1980.

86 Jausovec, N.: Hemispheric asymmetries during nine-year-olds' performance of divergent production tasks: A comparison of EEG and YSOLAT measures. *The Creative Child and Adult Quarterly*, 1985, **10**, pp. 233-238.

87 Konovalov, V. & Otmakhova, N.: EEG manifestations of functional asymmetry of the human cerebral cortex during perception of words and music. *Human Physiology*, 1984, **9**, pp. 250-255.

88 Levy, J.: Right brain, left brain: Fact and fiction. *Psychology Today*, May 1985, pp. 38-44.

89 Wilson, F.: Music as basic schooling for the brain. *Music Educators Journal*, May 1985, pp. 39-42.

90 Regelski, T.: *Arts Education and Brain Research*. Reston, VA: Music Educators National Conference, 1980.

91 Landreth, J. & Landreth H.: Effects of music on physiological response. *Journal of Research in Music Education*, 1974, **22**, pp. 4-12.

92 Goldstein, A.: Opioid peptides (endorphins) in pituitary and brain. *Science*, 1976, **193**, pp. 1081-1086.

93 Goldstein, A.: Thrills in response to music and other stimuli. *Physiological Psychology*, 1980, **8**, pp. 126-129.

94 Pribram, K.: Peptides and protocritic processes. In: L. Miller, C. Sandman, & A. Kaston (Eds.), *Neuropeptide Influences on the Brain and Behavior*. New York: Raven Press, 1977.

95 Alley, C.: The effect of relaxation training to music on heart rate and verbal reports. *Dissertation Abstracts International*, 1977, **37**, p. 6391-B.

96 Sime, W. & DeGood, D.: Effect of EMG biofeedback and progressive muscle relaxation training on awareness of frontalis muscle tension. *Psychophysiology*, 1977, **14**, pp. 522-530.

97 Barnes, L.: The effects of relaxation and music on stabilizing recall of didactic material. *Dissertation Abstracts International*, 1976, **37**, p. 1397-B.

98 Stoudenmire, J.: A comparison of muscle relaxation training and music in the reduction of state and trait anxiety. *Journal of Clinical Psychology*, 1975, **31**, pp. 490-492.

99 Peretti, P.: Changes in galvanic skin response as affected by muscle selection, sex, and academic discipline. *The Journal of Psychology*, 1975, **89**, pp. 183-187.

100 Peretti, P. & Swenson, K.: Effects of music in anxiety as determined by physiological skin responses. *Journal of Research in Music Education*, 1974, **22**, pp. 278-283.

101 Rohner, S. & Miller, R.: Degrees of familiar and affective music and their effects on state anxiety. *JMT*, 1980, **17**, p. 2-15.

102 Chetta, A.: The effect of music and desensitizaton on preoperative anxiety in children. *JMT*, 1981, **18**, pp. 74-87.

103 McFarland, R.: Relationship of skin temperature changes to the emotions accompanying music. *Biofeedback and Self-Regulation*, 1985, **10**, pp. 255-267.

104 Bonny, H.: Music listening for intensive care coronary units. *Music Therapy*, 1983, **3**, pp. 4-16.

105 Bonny, H. & Savery, L.: *Music and Your Mind*. New York: Harper and Row, 1973.

106 Peach, S.: Some implications for the clinical use of music facilitated imagery. *JMT*, 1984, **21**, pp. 27-34.

107 Quittner, A. & Gluekauf, R.: The facilitative effects of music on visual imagery: A multiple measures approach. *Journal of Mental Imagery*, 1983, **7**, pp. 105-119.

108 Rider, M.: Entrainment mechanisms involved in pain reduction, muscle relaxation, and music mediated imagery. *JMT*, 985, **22**, pp. 183-192.

109 Kibler, V. & Rider, M.: Effects of progressive muscle relaxation and music on stress as measured by finger temperature response. *Journal of Clinical Psychology*, 1983, **39**, pp. 213-215.

110 Wager, K.: *The Effects of Music, Imagery and Progressive Muscle Relaxation on Heart and Respiration Rates of Patients with Chronic Obstructive Pulmonary Disease*. Unpublished Manuscript, 1986.

111 Wolfe, D.: The effect of automated interrupted music on head posturing of cerebral palsied individuals. *JMT*, 1980, **17**, pp. 184-206.

112 Epstein, L., Hersen, M., & Hemphill, D.: Music feedback in the treatment of tension headache: An experimental case study. *Journal of Behavior Therapy and Experimental Psychiatry*, 1974, **5**, pp. 59-63.

113 Scartelli, J.: The effect of sedative music on electromyographic biofeedback assisted relaxation training of spastic cerebral palsied adults. *JMT*, 1982, **19**, pp. 210-218.

114 Gaston, E.: Dynamic music factors in mood change. *Music Educators Journal*, 1951, **37**, p. 42.

115 Scartelli, J.: The effect of EMG biofeedback and sedative music, EMG biofeedback only, and sedative music only on frontalis muscle relaxation ability. *JMT*, 1984, **21**, pp. 67-78.

116 Scartelli, J. & Borling, J.: The effects of sequenced versus simultaneous EMG biofeedback and sedative music on frontalis relaxation training. *JMT*, 1986, **23**, pp. 157-165.

117 Reynolds, S.: Biofeedback, relaxation training, and music: Homeostasis for coping with stress. *Biofeedback and Self-Regulation*, 1984, **9**, pp. 169-179.

118 Luria, A.: *The Working Brain: An Introduction to Neuropsychology.* New York: Basic Books, 1973.

119 Cook, R.: Left-right differences in the perception of dichotically presented music stimuli. *JMT*, 1973, **10**, pp. 59-63.

120 Budzynski, T.: Biofeedback and the twilight states of consciousness. In: G. Schwartz and D. Shapiro (Eds.), *Consciousness and Self-Regulation: Advances in Research.* New York: Plenum Press, 1976.

121 Budzynski, T.: Brain lateralization and rescripting. *Somatics,* Spring/Summer 1981, pp. 3-9.

122 Patterson, K.: *The Interaction of Instructional Set and Feedback Mode in the Acquisition of a Reduced Muscle Activity Response Via Biofeedback Training.* Ann Arbor: University Microfilms International, 1977.

123 Standley, J.: Music research in medical/dental treatment: Meta-analysis and clinical applications. *JMT*, 1986, **23**, pp. 56-122.

124 Farnsworth, P.: *The Social Psychology of Music,* 2nd ed. Ames, IA: Iowa State University Press, 1969.

125 Deutsch, D. (Ed.): *The Psychology of Music.* New York: Academic Press, 1982.

126 Radocy, R. & Boyle, J.: *Psychological Foundations of Musical Behavior.* Springfield, IL: Charles C. Thomas, 1979.

127 Harrer, G. & Harrer, H.: Music, emotion, and autonomic function. In: M. Critchley & R. Henson (Eds.), *Music and the Brain.* London: Heinemann Medical Books, 1977, pp. 206-216.

128 Taylor, D.: Subjective responses to precatagorized stimulative and sedative music. *JMT*, 1973, **10**, pp. 86-94.

129 Borling, J.: The effects of sedative music on alpha rhythms and focused attention in high-creative and low-creative subjects. *JMT*, 1981, **18**, pp. 101-108.

130 Stratton, V. & Zalinowski, A.: The relationship between music, degree of liking, and self-reported relaxation. *JMT*, 1984, **21**, pp. 184-192.

131 Smith, C. & Morris, C.: Differential effects of stimulative and sedative music in anxiety, concentration and performance. *Psychological Reports*, 1977, **41**, pp. 1047-1053.

132 Hanser, S., Larson, C. & O'Connell, A.: Music therapy assisted labor: Effects of relaxation of expectant mothers. *Birth Psychology Bulletin*, 1983, **4**, pp. 2-13.

133 Page, R. & Schaub, L.: EMG biofeedback applicability for differing personality types. *Journal of Clinical Psychology*, 1978, **34**, pp. 1014-1020.

134 Green, J. & Shellenberger, R.: Biofeedback research and the ghost in the box: A reply to Roberts. *American Psychologist,* September 1986, pp. 1003-1005.

135 McLeod, B.: Rx for health: A dose of confidence. *Psychology Today*, October 1986, pp. 46-50.

136 Weinman, M.: The effect of stressful life events on EMG biofeedback and relaxation training in the treatment of anxiety. *Biofeedback and Self-Regulation*, 1983, **8**, pp. 191-206.

137 Lloyd, R.: *Explorations in Psychoneuroimmunology.* Orlando, FL: Grune and Stratton, 1987.